# MESSIANIC
# PROPHECY
# REVEALED

Rabbi Kirt A. Schneider

# MESSIANIC
# PROPHECY
# REVEALED

CHARISMA
HOUSE

Visit the author's website at https://discoveringthejewishjesus.com.

Cataloging-in-Publication Data is on file with the Library of Congress.
International Standard Book Number: 978-1-63641-094-4
E-book ISBN: 978-1-63641-095-1

While the author has made every effort to provide accurate internet addresses at the time of publication, neither the publisher nor the author assumes any responsibility for errors or for changes that occur after publication. Further, the publisher does not have any control over and does not assume any responsibility for author or third-party websites or their content.

22 23 24 25 26 — 9 8 7 6 5 4 3 2 1
Printed in the United States of America

# Contents

# Acknowledgments

I WANT TO THANK Father and Yeshua for all my brothers and sisters whom I have gleaned from. To name each one would be very difficult because there are too many and I would accidentally leave some out.

To all the men and women of God who have been gifted with revelation by the Holy Spirit and have imparted something to me, I say, "*Todah rabah!*" (Great thanks!).

GOD'S SERVANT,
RABBI KIRT A. SCHNEIDER

## CHAPTER 1

# Hidden Prophecies of Jesus

THE BIBLICAL, HISTORICAL story of Yeshua, King Jesus, is bigger, grander, and more beautiful than many of us have imagined. It sweeps through the entire body of the Tanakh, which is the Hebrew Bible or what Christians know as the Old Testament. Through creation, through the Exodus, through the poetry of the Psalms and the pleading of the prophets, His story is revealed and told.

Of course, it is not novel to claim that Jesus fulfills the Old Testament. The Brit Chadashah (which is the Hebrew way to say the New Testament) repeatedly takes verses from the Hebrew Scriptures and tells us how Christ fulfilled them. Unfortunately, though, for many Christians the subject of how Jesus fulfills Messianic prophecy is often treated in a superficial and oversimplified way, causing it to be stripped of its full power, beauty, and meaning. It is not just the fact that Yeshua *does* fulfill the Hebrew Bible but *how* He fulfills it that transforms our understanding and roots us deeply in God's Word.

I recently heard a pastor say Messiah Jesus fulfills

three hundred prophecies from the Old Testament. His understanding, which is quite common, was that there are over three hundred scriptures in the Hebrew Bible that contain *future* predictions that can be scientifically measured that Messiah fulfilled. The problem is not that Jesus didn't fulfill these Messianic prophecies but rather *our understanding* of how He fulfilled them.

It is true that Yeshua fulfills highly particular Messianic prophecies in ways that are stunningly specific, as we will see. There are certainly very particular, measurable prophecies—for example, where Messiah would be born, His lineage, and His death—that we see fulfilled with specificity in the birth, life, death, and resurrection of Yeshua. But in the Hebrew tradition, prophecy is not one-dimensional; it is not simply foretelling the future in ways that can be scientifically verified. In reality, the whole of Scripture is multidimensionally prophetic, pointing us to Christ.

Many people have heard of the false prophet Nostradamus. He made specific predictions about the future that people anticipated coming to pass. So now, retrospectively, people claim Nostradamus predicted this flood, that earthquake, this war, and so on. Many Christians' view of Messianic prophecy limits it to functioning much the same way, as if Jesus merely fulfilled ancient Hebrew predictions about the future.

But Messianic prophecy is not simply the measurement of specific prophecies about the future that Yeshua fulfilled. This flat, one-dimensional way of thinking about Scripture in general and Messianic prophecy in particular is foreign to the rabbinic way and the approach to

Scripture that Messiah Jesus knew and practiced Himself. In fact, understanding Messianic prophecy involves both art and science, both poetry and math. I am proposing that to comprehend more fully how Yeshua is revealed in the Hebrew Bible, we need to be interpreting the Old Testament in a distinctly Jewish way. You see, to understand how Jesus fulfilled the Old Testament, we must open our minds to a Hebraic, Eastern way of thinking that is sometimes foreign to our Westernized mindset.

Rather than simply looking at how Yeshua fulfilled certain predictive Messianic prophecies, I want you to see that Jesus filled the entire Old Testament up with meaning. Take this in slowly, beloved: He filled it up with meaning. He carried the meaning of the Hebrew Scriptures to their fullest expression. This is why Messiah Jesus said, "Do not think that I came to abolish the Law or the Prophets; I did not come to abolish but to fulfill" (Matt. 5:17).

## OUT OF CONTEXT?

When I was in Bible school back in the eighties, I was confused by how the New Testament writers used the Old Testament to show how Yeshua fulfilled the Messianic prophecies. I remember specifically being in class studying Matthew chapter 2. We had just read of how the magi had seen the star in the east, signifying that the Savior had been born. When King Herod heard that the Messiah had been born, he viewed Him as a threat to his authority rather than as a source of hope. Afraid of losing his place, he ordered the slaughter of the Hebrew children under a year old. As a result of this death threat, an angel appeared to Joseph and told him to take the child Yeshua into Egypt. And that is what Joseph did.

But as powerful as Herod thought he was, even powerful men cannot avoid facing death, and the wicked king soon died. After Herod's death, God called Jesus and His family back to the land of Israel. Here is what happened:

> Behold, an angel of the Lord appeared to Joseph in a dream and said, "Get up! Take the Child and His mother and flee to Egypt, and remain there until I tell you; for Herod is going to search for the Child to destroy Him."
>
> So Joseph got up and took the Child and His mother while it was still night, and left for Egypt. He remained there until the death of Herod. *This was to fulfill what had been spoken by the Lord through the prophet: "Out of Egypt I called My Son."*
> —MATTHEW 2:13–15, EMPHASIS ADDED

Notice the last sentence in the passage: "This was to fulfill what had been spoken by the Lord through the prophet: 'Out of Egypt I called My Son.'" When we go to the Hebrew Bible, we find that there is only one place where the phrase "Out of Egypt I called My Son" is used: Hosea 11:1. In its historical context, this verse doesn't seem to be written as a prophecy. Rather, Hosea just seems to be speaking on the Lord's behalf, recounting Israel's history when he says, "When Israel was a youth

I loved him, and *out of Egypt I called My son*" (Hos. 11:1, emphasis added).

Again, in its initial historical context, this verse does not seem to be anticipating an event that was to be fulfilled in the future. Upon first reading, especially to ancient Israel, it was simply a powerful declaration from the Lord to the Israelites, His chosen people, about how He called them out of Egypt when He delivered them from Pharaoh. God was reminding Israel, His firstborn son (Exod. 4:22), of its history and what He had done for them.

So how does Matthew now say that Jesus fulfilled this? Specifically, how does Matthew say Hosea 11:1 was fulfilled when Joseph and Myriam (Mary) took Yeshua back into Israel from Egypt when in its initial context the verse was not a predictive, future prophecy to be fulfilled but rather a recounting of Israel's past?

This gets to the heart of why I say the subject of Messianic prophecy has been oversimplified. Much of the time, the way the New Testament speaks of Jesus' fulfillment of Messianic prophecy is not in the sense that He fulfilled some type of event the Hebrew people were looking forward to coming to pass. Rather, it is pointing to the fact that when Yeshua came, He filled Israel's history up by repeating it in His own life. Yeshua came and carried prophecies that were already fulfilled to their fullest meaning.

In the example from Hosea 11:1, God had already called Israel out of Egypt at the time Hosea wrote about it. He delivered His son Israel out of Egypt approximately thirteen hundred years before Jesus came. This wasn't an event people were expecting to happen; it had already happened. Yet again, Matthew quotes Hosea 11:1 claiming Yeshua fulfilled it. Why? Because Yeshua is Israel's divine representative and what Israel went through, Yeshua would also go through. So Matthew writes concerning Joseph's taking Yeshua back to Israel from Egypt, "This was to fulfill what had been spoken by the Lord through the prophet: 'Out of Egypt I called My Son'" (Matt. 2:15).

## MORE ART THAN SCIENCE

So you see, Messianic prophecy is more art than science, more poetry than math. The rabbinic way of reading Scripture is an art form. In order to more fully comprehend how the New Testament writers applied the Tanakh (Old Testament) to Jesus, I had to expand my perception and come outside my box. I needed to move outside my Western worldview where everything is linear—based on science and logic—and instead put myself in the mindset of Yeshua, Paul, and the other first-century Jewish writers of Scripture. In doing this, I have learned to apply the Scriptures in a way that is more deeply connected to the rabbinic tradition from which the Scriptures emerged.

Traditional rabbis don't apply the Scriptures to Yeshua, of course, but they take texts out of the Torah (the first five books of the Old Testament) and the Talmud (a collection of writings on Jewish law, custom, and religious practice) and give them a whole different type or level of meaning than what was evidenced in their initial historical or linear context. For example, today in Jewish institutes of learning called yeshivas, every student will study the Torah or Talmud with a partner. Every day the two students will sit across from each other and try to be as creative as possible in coming up with varying interpretations of the text they are studying. They will think of as many different meanings as they can, and the imagination is the limit.

In our rationalistic, modern Western culture, this way of using Scripture is considered "reading out of context." But in the ancient Jewish mind, as we see especially in the brilliant, Spirit-inspired genius of the apostle Paul, finding additional shades of meaning in a scripture was not novel. This is both the Jewish way and the tradition of Yeshua's times.

Now, I want to be clear that we are not free to give any interpretation to Scripture that we fancy. God, when He gave the Scriptures, knew exactly what He wanted to communicate to us. The correct interpretation is always the interpretation the Lord intends. I am simply helping you to understand how and why the New Testament writers applied the Scriptures from the Hebrew Bible to Yeshua in the way they did. God's purpose is to reveal His Son throughout the entirety of Scripture, and this is what both Yeshua and the New Testament writers did.

For example, in the case where Matthew quotes Hosea 11:1, traditional Orthodox Jews will say that Matthew misused the text. Their position as Orthodox Jews is that there is no way that Hosea could have been talking about Jesus. "Where did you get that interpretation?" they assert. "Hosea wasn't prophesying about the Messiah there." They would argue that Hosea was just giving us a historical, prophetic overview of Israel's history, of how God loved them and delivered them out of Egypt: "You Christians, you're just giving fanciful interpretations that have nothing to do with the original text."

But the reality is that the method of Scripture interpretation used by the New Testament writers is used in traditional Rabbinic Judaism all the time. As previously stated, for over two thousand years religious Jews have encouraged this dynamic, lively way of reading and studying God's Word. This multidimensional way of reading the Scriptures is the prophetic lens we need in order to discover the ways in which Yeshua fulfills the Hebrew Bible. You see, the Hebrew Bible is "full" of Him!

## THE STRANGER WALKS WITH US

To illustrate all that we have talked about, consider the events that unfolded following Yeshua's crucifixion. Two of Yeshua's disciples were walking from Jerusalem to Emmaus in utter despair. They had left everything to follow Him, and now He had been executed. Their faith was lost; their hearts were utterly broken. But in the very moment they were sharing their disillusionment and despair with each other, a "stranger" whom they did not recognize came alongside them.

The stranger asked, "What's going on?"

Almost indignantly they asked him, "Are you the only

one in the city who doesn't realize what just happened?" They began to pour out their hearts and their grief, sharing that their friend, teacher, and the One whom they followed as Messiah had been crucified. They were unaware that the stranger standing before them was the crucified One Himself.

In response, Yeshua, who appeared as a stranger to them, took them on a Bible study through the entire Tanakh. Starting from the top, from the Law of Moses (Genesis to Deuteronomy), all the way down through the Prophets and the Psalms, He gave them a stunning perspective, showing them how the Hebrew Scriptures pointing to the Messiah would be fulfilled. That day, as Yeshua spoke with the authority of One who contained every story within Himself, His two disciples discovered what the whole story had always been about. As Messiah Jesus blazed through the texts, He not only broke open the truth of the Scriptures; He broke open their minds and their very lives.

> Then beginning with Moses and with all the prophets, He explained to them the things concerning Himself in all the Scriptures....Now He said to them, "These are My words which I spoke to you while I was still with you, that all things which are written about Me in the Law of Moses and the Prophets and the Psalms must be fulfilled." Then He opened their minds to understand the Scriptures.
>
> —LUKE 24:27, 44–45

My hope as you read the pages ahead is that like those two disciples, you will see that Yeshua reveals Himself through the entire story of the Hebrew Scriptures.

As we close this chapter, let me say one more time that Messianic prophecy was never simply about Yeshua fulfilling some future anticipated event but rather about how He fills Israel's entire story with meaning. Jesus repeated and reenacted their history in His very body, thus filling Israel's history to its fullest in His own life, death, and resurrection. In the chapters ahead we will see Messianic prophecies wrapped in types and shadows. We will see Yeshua fulfill the ancient story as "the seed of Abraham," "the son of David," and the Messiah who would be born of a woman and bring God's light to the Gentiles. We will see how Yeshua is the true Lamb of God whom the Scriptures foretold.

By the time we get to the end of our study, you are going to both better understand the subject of Messianic prophecy and see what the disciples saw on that road to Emmaus (Luke 24:13–35)—that the entire Hebrew Bible paints a rich and colorful picture of King Yeshua and that He is the One who brings the story to its full and ultimate intent.

My prayer, though, is not only that Yeshua will reveal Himself to you through the prophecies of old, as He did with His disciples on the road to Emmaus, but that you will have a fresh revelation that He has been walking on the road of life with you all along—even when you did not recognize Him.

CHAPTER 2

# The Shadows of Messiah
# Jesus Revealed

WHEN WE READ the Hebrew Scriptures through the eyes of the first-century Jewish writers, we see that every story was pregnant with the hope of Messiah. The vivid stories of the patriarchs, the precision of the Levitical priests, the unrelenting passion of the prophets—all would culminate in the full revelation of Yeshua, the Word made flesh (John 1:1–5, 14). As previously stated, the apostle Paul and other writers of the New Testament were influenced by the rabbinic way and immersed in the imagery of the Hebrew Scriptures. So as they experienced the transformative power of Yeshua as their Messiah, they began to see Him within the ancient words of the Law of Moses, the Prophets, and the Psalms and realize He was the full embodiment of the Scriptures.

Messiah had been there all along, even in the very beginning. In language provocatively recalling Genesis, the Gospel of John powerfully and boldly proclaims, "In the beginning was the Word, and the Word was with God, and the Word was God" (John 1:1).

Indeed Yeshua is foreshadowed with stunning depth and clarity in the earliest and most celebrated Hebrew accounts, including the binding of Isaac, known in Hebrew as *Ha-Akedah*. We read about it in Genesis, called in Hebrew *Bereshit*, which means "in the beginning." This biblically epic story in Genesis 22 is fulfilled in Father God and Yeshua in sweeping and staggering ways that have implications for us all. People broadly know of this famous text as a story of sacrificial love— one in which Avraham, or Abraham, offers his beloved son Isaac to God. People will often rightly speak of the devotion and piety of Abraham here, of his total obedience and total surrender to God.

But as we go deeper into the narrative with a prophetic lens, this is a story of much more than just Abraham's devotion to God. Rather, Abraham himself functions as a prophetic type of God the Father. While Abraham had sons from other women, Isaac was his only son through his wife, Sarah. He was the son Abraham spent his whole life waiting for, the fulfillment of God's promise. Isaac, or Yitzchak in Hebrew, was the son born to him well past the age when he and his wife were naturally capable of producing children. All his hopes and dreams were bound up in this son, whose very existence was itself a miracle. Yet out of his unbridled, selfless love and fear of the Lord, Abraham freely offered Isaac up to God. It is a beautiful and passionate image of Father God's own extraordinary love for us, as He willingly offered up His only Son, with-holding nothing.

In this story, dense with layers of interpretive meaning, the typology unfolds even more deeply. When we see paintings of Abraham offering up Isaac as a sac-rifice, the art usually tells the same story—we see Isaac as a young boy, perhaps eleven years old or less. But according to Rabbinic Judaism, when Abraham offered up his son as a burnt offering, Isaac was not a little boy—he was thirty-seven years old! The moment you realize this, you know there is a much bigger picture. It is no longer a story of a small child led away without his con-sent to a fate outside his own reckoning.

Yes, it is very much a story of Abraham's absolute sur-render, but when you consider that Isaac was a thirty-seven-year-old man, he too is a hero of the story. You see, when we look at Isaac's own willingness to yield his life freely to his father in complete trust, we see an image of Messiah Jesus Himself foreshadowed in Isaac. Like Isaac, an adult who willingly offered up his life in obedience to his father, Abraham, so too does Yeshua willingly offer up His own life in obedience to Father God.

Surely for Isaac, coming to this place of surrender was excruciating. When we see Isaac, conscious of what he was doing and participating willingly with his father, we remember Messiah Yeshua just before He went to the cross, praying so intensely in the Garden of Gethsemane that blood came out the pores of His body. This was the agony of a man fully aware of Himself and of the pain that lay before Him. Feeling the full weight of the terror that lay ahead, He prayed, "Father, if You are willing, remove this cup from Me; yet not My will, but Yours be done" (Luke 22:42).

When we understand that Isaac was an adult who willingly offered himself as a sacrifice in obedience unto his father, we see in him a type of Messiah Yeshua in the clearest terms. While no sacrifice would be comparable to the one Jesus made when He gave Himself up for the sin of the world, Isaac, like Yeshua, knowingly offered up his own life on that altar, fully expecting to die there.

## A CHANNEL FOR GRACE

There is a second way rabbinic tradition opens us up to understand *Ha-Akedah*, the binding of Isaac, in an extraordinary way: Jewish thought teaches that this act opened up a channel for God's grace to be released upon Israel and the whole world. The rabbinic teaching is that before the binding of Isaac, God's grace was largely shut off from the earth. But Abraham's act of obedience and Isaac's act of radical surrender opened up a channel for the grace of God to come upon the nation of Israel, and through Israel to flood the entire world. The faithful sacrifice of the one (Isaac) opened up floodgates of mercy for the many.

As we have seen, the idea of an innocent one dying for the guilty and atonement being made through the innocent one's death is very much a part of both the Old and New Testaments. This concept of a righteous man, known in Hebrew as a *tzaddik*, dying in the place of the guilty was established in the rabbinic mind long before the New Testament was written. When we read the New Testament through the lens of the rabbinic mind, everything Yeshua says and does explodes with new meaning. I know by now you are appreciating how thoroughly Jewish the New Testament really is.

In the account of Abraham and Isaac, Isaac acts as a righteous representative who offers his life in place of the guilty. Even though he doesn't actually die, he was willing to die, and Abraham was willing to surrender him. So God accepted this sacrifice, and it opened up a channel of grace for future generations. We see this mindset, this same kind of rabbinic thinking, in the Brit Chadashah in John 11:49–51: "But one of them, Caiaphas, who was high priest that year, said to them, 'You know nothing at all, nor do you take into account that it is expedient for you that one man die for the people, and that the whole nation not perish.' Now he did not say this on his own initiative, but being high priest that year, he prophesied that [Yeshua] was going to die for the nation."

Again, this announcement within John's Gospel is nothing new; rather, it is an extension of the concept already at the heart of Israel's redemptive history: a righteous man could die on behalf of the nation, making atonement for the people and thereby opening up a channel of God's grace to the world. I have heard several accounts of people within today's Hasidic Jewish movement (an ultra-Orthodox Jewish movement whose spiritual leaders are called rebbes) who believe their rebbes can atone for the sins of Israel, stopping God's judgments by their own personal sacrifices. This is the notion the high priest in John 11 was prophesying about.

This theological concept is called propitiatory sacrificial atonement. It is the ancient notion that an innocent one can die in the place of the guilty and by virtue of that, the guilty are made righteous. Knowing what we know now, the words of Paul in 2 Corinthians 5:21 take on a much richer meaning: "He made Him who knew no sin to be sin on our behalf, so that we might become the righteousness of God in Him." Yeshua the innocent One took the weight of all our stories—all our sin and shame—into His very body. Yeshua released us from the guilt and consequences of our sin.

When you talk to people in today's Western culture, many of them believe in what they call karma, the idea that whatever you put out into the world comes back to you. And there is truth in the fact that we reap what we sow. But many who believe in karma go beyond our biblical understanding of sowing and reaping. New Age and Eastern religions teach that if you did bad things in this life, you will return in the next life as a lizard, a snake, or some other lower-level creature. Aren't you blessed to know Yeshua broke the karma, that He released you from having to come back as a rodent, that He released you from the ill-effects of your sin?

> Grace to you and peace, from Him who is and
> who was and who is to come, and from the seven
> Spirits who are before His throne, and from Jesus

Christ....To Him who loves us and *released us from our sins* by His blood.
—REVELATION 1:4–5, EMPHASIS ADDED

You have a clean slate. You're holy and blameless and righteous in Him because He, the innocent One, died in your place and shed His blood for you. You are washed; you are clean and stand blameless before God in His love. It's true that sometimes we suffer as a result of our actions. For example, if a man commits adultery and his wife divorces him and he is estranged from his children, this is, of course, a real hardship and consequence of sin. But I'm not talking about this. I'm talking about our relationship with our Creator. Through the blood of Jesus, we are accepted and loved by Him.

The apostle Paul wrote:

> Just as He chose us in Him before the foundation of the world, that we would be holy and blameless before Him. In love He predestined us to adoption as sons through Jesus Christ to Himself, according to the kind intention of His will, to the praise of the glory of His grace, which He freely bestowed on us in the Beloved. In Him we have redemption through His blood, the forgiveness of our trespasses, according to the riches of His grace.
> —EPHESIANS 1:4–7

So continuing on, the binding of Isaac not only foreshadows Yeshua's sacrificial death but it also points to His resurrection. In Genesis 22, Abraham is just about to leave the base of Mount Moriah to take Isaac to the top, where he plans to put him to death. This would seem to be a moment of unspeakable grief. But just before he leaves, Abraham says something peculiar to his servants: "Stay here with the donkey, and I and the lad will go over there; and we will worship and return to you" (Gen. 22:5). How is it that as he is on the precipice of offering his only son as a sacrifice, he simultaneously assures his servants that they will both return?

It is not that Abraham was merely being optimistic. Abraham spoke those words knowing that God would surely also raise Isaac from the dead. In addition to Yeshua's death being prophetically shadowed in the story of Abraham and Isaac, so too is Yeshua's resurrection. The writer of the New Testament Book of Hebrews says:

> By faith Abraham, when he was tested, offered up Isaac...his only begotten son....*He considered that God is able to raise people even from the dead, from which he also received him back as a type.*
> —Hebrews 11:17, 19, emphasis added

The Book of Hebrews clearly reveals that Isaac was a type of Yeshua's resurrection.

## The Rejection and Exaltation of Joseph

One of the most colorful personalities in the Tanakh is Yosef, or Joseph. As you may know, Joseph was Jacob's favorite son. Jacob made him an elegant, multicolored garment, an ornate sign of his affection that only made his brothers seethe all the more in their resentment of him. Joseph's brothers so burned with jealousy against him that they plotted to get rid of him once and for all. They schemed to kill him by throwing him into a pit, but changed their minds, deciding instead to sell him as a slave to the Ishmaelites. This is how Joseph eventually found himself in Egypt as a slave. This son who was the object of his father's delight was rejected by his own brothers, betrayed, and given up to a cruel fate, seemingly to be forgotten. It is a story that would seem to have ended in a cruel tragedy.

Yet despite the fact that Joseph was betrayed and abandoned by his own flesh and blood, the grace of Yahweh was so powerful on him that though he started out as a slave, he kept rising up through the ranks until he ultimately became second-in-command in Egypt. God used him to literally save the Egyptians from starving to death during a famine. Joseph's entire story is a wonder and an adventure, but here is where it particularly becomes a foreshadowing of Messiah Jesus. Joseph was originally rejected by his brothers, but he became the savior of the Egyptians. Then later he became the savior of his brothers as well.

Just like Joseph, Yeshua would be rejected by His own people but bring salvation to the Gentiles. Consider again: After being rejected by his brothers, Joseph saved the Egyptians. Later, his brothers went to Egypt to buy grain because of the severe famine they were experiencing in their land, Canaan. While in Egypt, Joseph revealed himself to them and brought them to live there, literally saving them from starving to death. This is a staggeringly specific foreshadowing of King Jesus, who was originally rejected by His own flesh-and-blood brothers, the Jews, but was received by the Gentiles, saving them.

So once again, Joseph first saved Egypt. It was only afterward that he saved his brothers (when they went to Egypt to buy grain because they were starving to death). Consider the prophetic pattern. First Joseph saved the Gentiles (Egypt) and then later saved his own flesh-and-blood brothers. In the same way, Yeshua is currently saving Gentiles around the world, and yet the eyes of His own flesh and blood remain largely closed.

Think about this in relation to Paul's words in the Book of Romans:

> For I do not want you, brethren, to be uninformed of this mystery—so that you will not be wise in your own estimation—*that a partial hardening has happened to Israel until the fullness of the Gentiles has come in; and so all Israel will be saved*; just as it is written, "The Deliverer will come from Zion, He will remove ungodliness from Jacob."
> —ROMANS 11:25–26, EMPHASIS ADDED

Zechariah similarly wrote about the salvation of the Jewish people at the end of the age: "I will pour out on the house of David and on the inhabitants of Jerusalem, the Spirit of grace and of supplication, so that they will look on Me whom they have pierced; and they will mourn for Him, as one mourns for an only son" (Zech. 12:10).

Looking further at the life of Joseph, we see that as a result of living in Egypt, this Hebrew son began to look more and more like an Egyptian. He dressed in Egyptian clothes and wore Egyptian makeup. Eventually Joseph no longer looked like a Hebrew; he looked like an Egyptian. In fact, when Joseph's brothers went to Egypt to buy grain, Joseph looked so much like an Egyptian that his brothers didn't even recognize him. In the same way, today Yeshua is being portrayed not as a Jew but as a Gentile. As a result, it is preventing Jewish people from recognizing Him as their Messiah.

We see this clearly in much of the most enduring, iconic Western art depicting Yeshua. In Leonardo da Vinci's celebrated painting of Jesus at the Last Supper, Jesus bears no resemblance to a Jew. He has no traces of His Middle Eastern descent. He is instead a fair-skinned, Scandinavian-looking man with red hair, wearing a blouse of some sort. This aristocratic, European Jesus is not a Jesus His own people would recognize. He looks like a Gentile man with no connection to the culture, bloodlines, or traditions of the Jewish people of His origin.

As a result, many of God's first-covenant people are blocked from seeing Jesus as the King of the Jews, their Messiah. But the time will come when, as Joseph took off his makeup and revealed himself to his brothers, Yeshua HaMashiach will likewise be revealed for who He really is to His flesh-and-blood brothers (Rom. 9:3–5), the children of Israel.

Furthermore, consider that Joseph found himself in

Egypt because of his own brothers' rejection of him. In the same way, the gospel of Yeshua has spread to the Gentiles because His own people rejected Him. "He came unto his own, and his own received him not" (John 1:11, KJV).

After his vision of Jesus, Paul the apostle was convinced that God was going to use him to bring his own people to faith in the Messiah. He thought he was the perfect candidate to bring the message of Messiah Jesus to his fellow Jews. Paul said this about himself: "If anyone else has a mind to put confidence in the flesh, I far more: circumcised the eighth day, of the nation of Israel, of the tribe of Benjamin, a Hebrew of Hebrews; as to the Law, a Pharisee" (Phil. 3:4–5). Paul saw himself as one who was totally qualified and equipped to reach his own people. But instead, God spoke to him while he was in the Temple and directed him otherwise.

> It happened when I returned to Jerusalem and was praying in the temple, that I fell into a trance, and I saw Him saying to me, "Make haste, and get out of Jerusalem quickly, because they will not accept your testimony about Me." And I said, "Lord, they themselves understand that in one synagogue after another I used to imprison and beat those who believed in You. And when the blood of Your witness Stephen was being shed, I also was standing by approving, and watching out for the coats of those who were slaying him." And He said to me, "Go! For I will send you far away to the Gentiles."
> —ACTS 22:17–21

So again as it was in the case of Joseph, we see the same pattern, where God's messenger is first rejected by his own people and as a result is sent to the Gentiles. After the Gentiles respond, God's first-covenant people experience Yahweh's salvation.

Many of the patriarchs in the Hebrew Bible have journeys that foreshadowed the Messiah. This is precisely why on the road to Emmaus, Yeshua took those first disciples of His on a journey through the entire Torah, the Prophets, and the Psalms, showing them Himself in "all the Scriptures" (Luke 24:27).

The details of these respective stories are as colorful and varied as the patriarchs themselves. But in their diversity we see an essential unity emerge: they all bear witness to Him. Consider the time when Yeshua referred back to the Book of Numbers, referencing the story of Moses lifting up a serpent on a staff to the children of Israel, who were dying because they were being bitten by serpents as a penalty for their sin. In this biblical narrative, Moses told the children of Israel that if they would look at the serpent atop the staff he was holding, they would be saved. This too was a type of Messianic prophecy. Yeshua said to His Jewish hearers, "As Moses *lifted up* the serpent in the wilderness, even so must the Son of Man be *lifted up*; so that whoever believes will in Him have eternal life" (John 3:14–15, emphasis added).

Jesus would be lifted by hanging on an actual execution stake (the cross) above the people on the ground so they could see Him. Roman crosses were approximately nine to twelve feet high, and the average Jewish male of Jesus' day was five feet five inches in height (the same as me, which makes me feel a little better about being short). Jesus was lifted up above the people on the ground at His crucifixion. And He is lifted up today whenever His gospel is preached in the power and fire of the Ruach HaKodesh and wherever His people are leading holy lives.

As a side note, the serpent on the staff lifted up for healing is an extremely powerful, enduring symbol. Many believe this story in Numbers 21:6–9 is where we get our present-day medical symbol—which depicts serpents wrapped around a pole.

As we come to better see these shadows and types in the Hebrew Bible fulfilled in the person, nature, and ministry of Yeshua, our faith is increased and we open ourselves up to deeper experiences of His healing and saving power.

# CHAPTER 3

# The Blood of the Lamb

A s we have seen, the Scriptures have multiple levels of revelation and meaning, as is the case in Hosea 11:1, which we examined in chapter 1. Giving scriptures manifold layers of meaning is not a novelty that originates with the New Testament. Rather, it is the traditional rabbinic way of interpretation through which the Hebrew Bible has always been understood by religious Jews. In fact, Rabbinic Judaism assigns four levels of reading or understanding to the Hebrew Bible.

The first is called *peshat*; this is simply the plain, intended meaning of the text. The second level of reading or understanding is called *remez*. This refers to alluded meaning beyond the literal sense; it's the allegorical or symbolic meaning the text hints at when you read between the lines. The third level is called *derash*; this is a method of interpretation that seeks to uncover a deeper meaning of the passage by examining the words of the text and looking at where those same words are used elsewhere in Scripture.

Finally, the fourth and deepest level of interpretation

is called *sod*, which seeks to find a mystical or esoteric meaning in the text. I don't want to go off on a detour with all this. I just want to reiterate that the way the New Testament writers used the Hebrew Scriptures and applied them to Yeshua is totally within the rabbinic framework.

In this chapter, I want to look at types and shadows in the Tanakh that are discovered beneath the surface and that point to Yeshua. These are broad-brush biblical stories full of depth, color, and meaning that foreshadow Yeshua and symbolically point to Him.

## BLOOD IN THE HEBREW BIBLE

Let's begin with the concept of blood in the Hebrew Bible. The unfolding river of Israel's story flows with currents of redemption, grace, and beauty, and yet there was always a great cost—a tide that flows red with blood. Blood is significant in the Hebrew Bible, not because it points to moments of horror or cruelty but simply because of its essence.

In the Book of Leviticus (*Vayikra* in Hebrew) the Scriptures say, "*The life of the flesh is in the blood,* and I have given it to you on the altar to make atonement for your souls; for *it is the blood by reason of the life that makes atonement*" (Lev. 17:11, emphasis added). Blood is at the center of Israel's story because it is at the center of life itself—"The life of the flesh is in the blood." Even before we learned of the unique power in Yeshua's blood, one of the particular insights gained from the Hebrew religion is the understanding that the power or essence of life is quite literally in the blood.

We often think that our life force is bound to the physical human heart. For example, when someone's heart stops beating, we pronounce that person dead. Some think our life center is in our minds, which is why when someone's brain stops functioning after a traumatic injury, that person is often taken off life support. But the Creator says that the life of the flesh is in the blood.

The fact is that the importance of blood is seen throughout the entire Hebrew Bible. Israel's birth as a nation took place when God delivered them out of Egypt. And how did God deliver the Israelites out of Egypt? It was through the blood of the lamb that they applied to the doorposts.

After the Lord took the Israelites out of Egypt through the blood of the lamb and brought them to Mount Sinai, Moses spent forty days and forty nights on top of the mountain. There he received Yahweh's divine revelation and covenant. Then he came down from the mountain and assembled all the Israelites before him to communicate the words that Yahweh had spoken. After Moses communicated God's covenant to them, the Israelites responded, "All that the LORD has spoken we will do!" (Exod. 19:8). Following this solemn, historic moment when the Israelites accepted the covenant, Moses sprinkled them with blood (Exod. 24:8).

Why are we tracing a line of blood all the way through the Hebrew Bible when we are focusing on Messianic prophecy? Because Yeshua's ministry climaxed with the shedding of His blood. All these incidents of blood in the Hebrew Bible were pointing to Yeshua and help us to understand who He is and what He has done for us.

As this blood-covered story of redemption in the Hebrew Bible continues to unveil toward an inevitable climax, Moses teaches the Israelites about certain holy days that must be celebrated to honor Yahweh. He gave them a calendar around which the entire life of the community of God would be oriented. Within that calendar, the highest and holiest day is Yom Kippur, the Day of Atonement. In the Book of Leviticus, chapter 16, the Lord gave precise instructions to Moses about how Yom Kippur was to be celebrated. The priest needed to take the blood of both a bull and a goat inside the most sacred place on earth, the Holy of Holies, located in the Tabernacle (which was later developed into the permanent Temple in Jerusalem).

Inside the Holy of Holies was the Ark of the Covenant, and inside the Ark of the Covenant were the Ten Commandments. On Yom Kippur, the high priest took the blood of the bull and the goat, brought it into the Holy of Holies, and sprinkled it on top of the Ark of the Covenant, often referred to as the Mercy Seat. Then, when the Lord saw the blood of the innocent animal on top of the Ark of the Covenant, He forgave the sins of the children of Israel. To stress this point again—"the life of the flesh is in the blood," and the Lord gave it to us "to make atonement for [our] souls" (Lev. 17:11).

Do you see why Jesus had to die on the cross and shed His blood—why it was so crucial for that spear to be thrust in His side, causing His blood to flow? It was so atonement could be made. The Hebrew Bible had telegraphed this with the blood of the Passover lamb, the blood Moses sprinkled Israel with at the base of Mount Sinai, and the blood that was applied to the Mercy Seat on Yom Kippur. The only way man has access to God is when blood is shed. On the cross, an innocent One yielded His blood and died in the place of the guilty. All the sacrifices of the Hebrew Bible—all the blood that was spilled—was a shadow that was fulfilled by Messiah Yeshua.

## THE NECESSITY OF A MEDIATOR

It was not just the sacrifice itself that mattered. The one who offered it and the place it was offered are critical components as well. Specifically, from the very beginning, forgiveness and reconciliation to the one true God would require a God-appointed priest and mediator. The Israelites had to offer their sacrifices through a priest in order for their sacrifices to be accepted. This concept is first illustrated in the Torah through Abraham, who offered his tithe through the priest Melchizedek (Gen. 14:20), and is further seen in the fact that once the Law was given, the Israelites had to present their sacrifices through the Levitical priesthood. Individual Israelites could only approach the Lord through the God-appointed priesthood.

We see how Yeshua fulfilled both the mysterious priesthood of Melchizedek as well as the Levitical priesthood. In relation to Melchizedek, the Scripture says he was "without father, without mother, without genealogy, having neither beginning of days nor end of life, but made like the Son of God, he remains a priest perpetually" (Heb. 7:3). In other words, he was a shadow of Christ.

In relation to the Levitical priesthood, we read in Hebrews 6 through 10 how specifically Yeshua has both fulfilled and replaced the Levitical priesthood. The Torah clearly reveals that humanity can only approach their Creator via a mediator-priesthood.

On this same subject the New Testament says, "There is one God, and one mediator also between God and men, the man Christ Jesus" (1 Tim. 2:5). Jesus has become for us both our offering and our priest/mediator.

> Therefore, brethren, since we have confidence to enter the holy place by the blood of Jesus, by a new and living way which He inaugurated for us through the veil, that is, His flesh, and since we have a great priest over the house of God, let us draw near with a sincere heart in full assurance of faith.
> —HEBREWS 10:19–22

In the Hebrew Bible the Lord told the children of Israel to build a Tabernacle, called in Hebrew a *Mishkan*. All around the *Mishkan* were walls. There was only one way, one door to enter the Tabernacle, where the presence of the Lord dwelled. You couldn't just wander in from any direction. You had to enter in through the one and only door. Similarly, Yeshua said unequivocally, "I am the door; if anyone enters through Me, he will be saved" (John 10:9).

Again, if people wanted to meet with God in the Hebrew Bible, they had to come to the *Mishkan*, the Tabernacle, and enter through its one door. They had to present their offering through a priest. And they needed a blood sacrifice. Yeshua fulfilled all these types and shadows.

Early in His ministry, Messiah confused and infuriated the religious leaders when He said, "'Destroy this temple, and in three days I will raise it up.' The Jews then said, 'It took forty-six years to build this temple, and will You raise it up in three days?' But He was speaking of the temple of His body" (John 2:19–21). Then He later said, "Do you see this temple? Not one stone will be left standing":

> And while some were talking about the temple, that it was adorned with beautiful stones and votive gifts, He said, "As for these things which you are looking at, the days will come in which there will not be left one stone upon another which will not be torn down."
>
> —LUKE 21:5–6

At the end of His ministry, when Jesus stood on trial before the high priest, He was lambasted, with this charge made against Him:

> They led Jesus away to the high priest; and all the chief priests and the elders and the scribes gathered together....Now the chief priests and the whole Council kept trying to obtain testimony

> against Jesus to put Him to death, and they were
> not finding any....Some stood up and began to
> give false testimony against Him, saying, "We
> heard Him say, 'I will destroy this temple made
> with hands, and in three days I will build another
> made without hands.'"
>
> —MARK 14:53, 55, 57–58

The religious establishment didn't realize Jesus was talking about His own body and that He Himself would become the Temple.

Yeshua has become "the place." He has become the One we must go through if we are going to have fellowship with Father God. Even as Israel of old came to the ancient Temple, which has been destroyed for about two thousand years now, so too in order for us to have fellowship with God, we need to come not to bricks and stone but to the One who *is* the Temple.

We read in Matthew that as soon as Yeshua died from the crucifixion, the veil in the Temple that separated the Holy of Holies, where God's visible and manifest presence resided, ripped in two.

> And Jesus cried out again with a loud voice, and
> yielded up His spirit. And behold, the veil of the
> temple was torn in two from top to bottom; and
> the earth shook and the rocks were split.
>
> —MATTHEW 27:50–51

This phenomenon revealed that it was no longer the physical Temple made of stone through which man had access to God; Messiah Yeshua had become the way.

> Therefore, brethren, since we have confidence to enter the holy place by the blood of Jesus, by a new and living way which He inaugurated for us through the veil, that is, His flesh, and since we have a great priest over the house of God, let us draw near with a sincere heart in full assurance of faith.
>
> —HEBREWS 10:19–22

The uniqueness of Yeshua cannot be overstated. We are living in a culture today that puts tremendous pressure on believers to conform to cultural norms of political correctness that teaches that all paths lead to God and that we have no right to push our faith in Jesus on anybody. "Your faith is no better than my faith," it claims. "Your path is the same as my own; you are just taking a different way." Although this mindset is politically correct and even sounds polite, it is completely wrong and unbiblical. The Hebrew Scriptures have always borne witness to one God who made Himself known to His people in a specific way. The story of this one and only God reaches its inevitable and inescapable climax, with searing specificity, in the person of Yeshua.

When you understand the unambiguous and clear-cut ways Yeshua fulfilled Messianic prophecy and His claims to be the only way to salvation, you aren't going to be able to take a position that says, "Jesus is good for me, but I respect all religious paths." You are going to know that either Yeshua is the only way or He's no way at all. Either He is the Savior of everyone or He is the Savior of no one because He claimed to be the only way. As C. S. Lewis famously said, He's either a liar, a lunatic, or the Lord. Do you understand? When Yeshua said, "No one can come to the Father except through me" (John 14:6, NLT), He was either consciously lying to His hearers, He was crazy (He thought He was the Messiah but He wasn't, like someone in a psychiatric hospital), or He was who He said He was—the Messiah and the one and only way into a relationship with the Creator.

Messianic prophecy grounds us. In a culture that is teaching that everybody has his or her own path to God and we need to leave everyone alone and stop witnessing for our Messiah Jesus, we say emphatically, "No!"

# CHAPTER 4
# Fulfilling Israel's Destiny

IN JOHN 13:18, Yeshua quotes Psalm 41:9 and says, "He who eats My bread has lifted up his heel against Me." Yeshua was drawing attention to how Judas was going to betray Him. The words He quoted were familiar to His listeners—they knew this as a line from the Psalms, the hymnal and prayer book of the Hebrew Bible. The psalm Jesus quoted were words first spoken by David, Israel's most celebrated king, while he was experiencing his own personal betrayal. David was most likely not thinking about Yeshua when he wrote the psalm nor intending to make a prediction about how Jesus would one day be betrayed by one of His friends. Why, then, would the Jewish apostle Yochanan (the Hebrew way to say *John*) take this psalm of David, apply it to Jesus, and say He fulfilled it?

To understand this dilemma, we must return to the mindset of the Jews of Yeshua's day. They didn't approach the Scriptures one-dimensionally. The writers of the New Testament are not suggesting that Yeshua fulfilled a prediction about the future but rather that

Jesus once again brought Israel's destiny to fulfillment in Himself. The same things that happened to Israel historically happened to Jesus in His own life. Yeshua, as Israel's divine representative, repeated the same things Israel and its key leaders went through in their history.

As I mentioned before, when the New Testament writers speak about how Jesus fulfilled many scriptures in the Old Testament, they are not necessarily saying Jesus fulfilled a prediction but are referring to how Jesus filled up Israel's story with meaning. This is why in Luke 24, when Jesus was walking the road to Emmaus with two disillusioned disciples who did not yet recognize Him, He said: "'O foolish men and slow of heart to believe in all that the prophets have spoken!...All things which are written about Me in the Law of Moses and the Prophets and the Psalms must be fulfilled.' Then He opened their minds to understand the Scriptures" (vv. 25, 44–45). The truth of Messiah was already in the texts, but it had to be *revealed.* Yeshua took them on an incredible journey through the Tanakh, unlocking its hidden mysteries.

Buried deep beneath the surface of the Scriptures were prophecies that pointed to Jesus but were not immediately evident as Messianic prophecies at the time they were written. This is why Jesus had to show His apostles how many of the events that took place in the Hebrew Bible and in the lives of the prophets were actually foreshadowing His own life and ministry.

In Acts 8:32–33 we see a similar phenomenon when we find an Ethiopian eunuch, a court official of Candace, queen of the Ethiopians, reading Isaiah's achingly beautiful words:

> He was led as a sheep to slaughter; and as a lamb
> before its shearer is silent, so He does not open
> His mouth. In humiliation His judgment was
> taken away; who will relate His generation? For
> His life is removed from the earth.

According to Levitical law, eunuchs were considered ceremonially unclean because the Law of Moses specifically forbids people from crushing or mutilating their genitals. In ancient times, men were sometimes voluntarily and sometimes involuntarily castrated in order to serve in the official court of a queen, so there would be no danger they would try to force the birth of an unintended heir. It was a way ancient people tried to protect the throne. People who had undergone such a procedure were considered disqualified from holy places and holy things. But this Ethiopian eunuch was a devout man who worshipped the true God of the Hebrews, and he desired to understand the truth of the prophet's words he was reading.

While the Ethiopian eunuch was in the very act of pondering all this, God supernaturally sent Philip to him. God moved Philip from the throes of a remarkable revival, where he was seeing throngs of people delivered and healed in the name of Yeshua, all for the sake of this one outcast man, who was riding on an obscure, desolate desert road.

Philip asked the man, "Do you understand what you are reading?" And he responded, "How can I, unless someone guides me?" This should help us to realize that the revelation of Yeshua is not clear and obvious to everyone who reads the Hebrew Scriptures. Sometimes, like this Ethiopian eunuch, we also need to be guided and have someone come alongside us to open the texts for us. At one time or another we need someone like Philip to help us understand the deeper meaning of the text. That is my hope for you as you read now—that you will sense the Hebrew Scriptures being opened up to you.

## TYPOLOGICAL PROPHECY

We will now turn our attention to studying the concept of typological prophecy. Typological prophecy is when a prophecy has already been fulfilled historically and then is fulfilled again in a more intense way. It could be compared to a pregnant woman who has mild contractions hours before feeling the full force of the labor pains. Although labor began with her first pain, it didn't end with her first pain. The pains repeated themselves and grew in intensity. Typological prophecies are not just fulfilled once; they are fulfilled again, finding their ultimate fulfillment in the person of King Jesus and His ministry.

For example, in Isaiah 7:14, the prophet says, "Therefore the Lord Himself will give you a sign: Behold, a virgin will be with child and bear a son, and she will call His name Immanuel." Traditional rabbis argue that this verse does not apply to Jesus but rather to the son of

Isaiah himself. (Other traditional Jewish sources ponder whether this prophecy anticipated the birth of Hezekiah, who was the son of Ahaz, the king of Israel.) Either way, in both of these instances, traditional Rabbinic Jews maintain that Isaiah 7:14 was already fulfilled.

But Matthew quotes Isaiah 7:14 in reference to Yeshua. (See Matthew 1:23.) Matthew claims that the virgin (Mary) has conceived and given us a child (Yeshua), called Immanuel, meaning "God with us," and that this is the fulfillment of Isaiah's words. In other words, although Matthew is aware that Isaiah 7:14 had already been fulfilled through the birth of Isaiah's or Ahaz's son, the *ultimate* fulfillment of this scripture is in the person and the birth of Messiah Jesus.

The fact is, Isaiah did have a son, and so did Ahaz. Typological prophecy does not deny that certain prophecies have already been fulfilled historically in a measurable way—only that they had not yet been fulfilled in the fullest sense. The New Testament writers declare that Messiah Jesus has brought these typological prophecies to the pinnacle of fulfillment.

Let's consider another example of this, when Abraham, the first believer, was promised a son.

> Now the LORD appeared to him by the oaks of Mamre, while he was sitting at the tent door in the heat of the day....He said, "I will surely return to you at this time next year; and behold, Sarah your wife will have a son." And Sarah was listening at the tent door, which was behind him.

> Now Abraham and Sarah were old, advanced in age; Sarah was past childbearing.
>
> Sarah laughed to herself, saying, "After I have become old, shall I have pleasure, my lord being old also?" And the LORD said to Abraham, "Why did Sarah laugh, saying, 'Shall I indeed bear a child, when I am so old?' Is anything too difficult for the LORD? At the appointed time I will return to you, at this time next year, and Sarah will have a son."
>
> —GENESIS 18:1, 10–14

Think about how Abraham's own son, Isaac, was born. He was conceived supernaturally, born to a ninety-year-old woman and her one hundred-year-old husband. Far past the age of childbearing, when it was utterly impossible for Sarah to give birth biologically, she miraculously had a son, Isaac. The Lord's prophecy to Abraham and Sarah was fulfilled with the supernatural birth of Isaac. (I will go into more detail on this subject in chapter 7.)

This typological pattern of supernatural birth is climaxed in the birth of Yeshua, who was brought into the world in the most extreme, supernatural way of all. A literal virgin gave Him birth. What had happened in the Hebrew Scriptures through the miraculous birth of Isaac through a woman who was in the natural unable to conceive due to her old age pointed to Messiah Jesus, who was born in the most extreme and ultimate supernatural way of all—through a virgin!

Here is another example of typological prophecy: In Daniel 11:31, Daniel speaks of an Antichrist who will rise up to oppose the Messiah and the kingdom of heaven.

Daniel says he "will arise, desecrate the sanctuary fortress, and do away with the regular sacrifice. And they will set up *the abomination of desolation*" (Dan. 11:31, emphasis added; see also Daniel 9:27). This phrase, "the abomination of desolation," is used by Yeshua in Matthew 24:15, when He tells us that He will return "when you see *the abomination of desolation* which was spoken of through the prophet Daniel" (emphasis added).

Here again, traditional rabbis tell us this prophecy from Daniel about the abomination of desolation was fulfilled approximately seven hundred years after Daniel's prophecy with the person of Antiochus Epiphanes. In approximately 168 BC, Antiochus IV went into God's Temple in Jerusalem and desecrated it by sacrificing a pig— the most unholy animal on the planet—to the pagan deity Zeus. Traditional Judaism teaches that this act was the abomination of desolation—and it was! A pagan god was worshipped and sacrificed to in the holy Jewish Temple.

So how does Yeshua say that before His return, the abomination of desolation Daniel spoke of will yet take place?

It is not that the prophecy wasn't fulfilled in a prior historical event but rather that the full meaning of the prophecy hadn't reached its climax. It found initial fulfillment when Antiochus Epiphanes desecrated the Temple, but it will find its ultimate fulfillment at the end of the age when the Antichrist succeeds in creating a false world religion in the earth.

Ultimately, God is going to break in and judge the anti-Messiah, and the fire of God will eradicate evil from the earth. So we see once again that typological prophecy is prophecy that was fulfilled before Jesus came, in this case with Antiochus Epiphanes (whose name, by the way, means "God Manifest"[1]), but will be fulfilled again in the ultimate sense when the Antichrist creates a false world religion—the abomination of desolation—before Yeshua returns.

This should prepare you for it: At some point in your life you quote a Messianic prophecy to a Jewish person, and they say to you in response, "The New Testament says your Jesus fulfilled that verse, but if you look at the scripture in the original Hebrew Bible, your interpretation is not what that scripture was talking about." We are accused of taking a scripture that had one meaning to the original author and, out of context, applying it to Jesus. "That is not an authentic use of the Tanakh," they will say.

My internal response to this accusation is that this is an accurate and honest use of Scripture because I am confident that the writers of the New Testament were under the inspiration of the Holy Spirit. "But know this first of all, that no prophecy of Scripture is a matter of one's own interpretation, for no prophecy was ever made by an act of human will, but men moved by the Holy Spirit spoke from God" (2 Pet. 1:20–21). Yeshua is the Messiah, and we can and should use the Scriptures to point to Him, feeling fully confident and convinced that we are using the Scriptures accurately. The point of the Scriptures all along, beloved, was to bring us to Him!

## GOD WITH US

Upon closing this chapter, let's further consider the words we examined from Isaiah 7:14: we "will call His name Immanuel," which means "God with us." The full meaning of "God with us" is still unfolding in our lives today. These living, breathing words are not just about the past, though they had deep meaning in the past. They are also not entirely about the future, though they have profound implications for the future. Rather, they also reveal the God who is here for us right here, right now.

Many people are still looking for God someplace "out there," as though if we could somehow see far enough into space, we might be able to connect with Him. But the truth is, God is already here. The problem is not that God is so far away that we can't get to Him, but that God is so close we are often too afraid or prideful to let Him in! Immanuel is not stuck in the past or bound to some distant future. The God who is revealed through Yeshua is with us currently.

After Yeshua ascended to heaven, He sent the Ruach HaKodesh, the breath of Elohim (God):

> I will ask the Father, and He will give you another Helper, that He may be with you forever....The Helper, the Holy Spirit, whom the Father will send in My name, He will teach you all things, and bring to your remembrance all that I said to you. Peace I leave with you; My peace I give to

you; not as the world gives do I give to you. Do not let your heart be troubled, nor let it be fearful.
—JOHN 14:16, 26–27

But when He, the Spirit of truth, comes, He will guide you into all the truth; for He will not speak on His own initiative, but whatever He hears, He will speak; and He will disclose to you what is to come. He will glorify Me, for He will take of Mine and will disclose it to you. All things that the Father has are Mine; therefore I said that He takes of Mine and will disclose it to you.
—JOHN 16:13–15

That Spirit is here with us on the earth. This is how Jesus could say, "I am with you always, even to the end, and I'll never leave you or forsake you." (See Matthew 28:20 and Deuteronomy 31:6.) He is and has been with us throughout our entire lives and continues to say, "Behold, I stand at the door and knock; if anyone hears My voice and opens the door, I will come in to him and will dine with him, and he with Me" (Rev. 3:20).

Perhaps right now you are feeling anxiety and stress and that all the pressures of life are closing in on you. Maybe you are feeling anxiety from the relationships and circumstances in which you find yourself. But I want to say to you, beloved one—God is here, and Yeshua wants to ground you in this reality!

This is why David could say, "Even though I walk through the valley of the shadow of death, I fear no evil, for You are with me" (Ps. 23:4). Sometimes we feel like we are groping in the darkness. But I want to ask you to affirm this simple truth with me: "God is here."

The fact that God is here doesn't mean life is going to be easy. What it means is as we practice the presence of God—as we affirm the truth that God is present and lovingly trust Him—the roots of our soul grow deep in the soil of the Holy Spirit. As our souls are rooted in the reality of the nearness of God, we become stronger, more peaceful, and more joyful.

In addition to information about Yeshua and all the ways He has fulfilled prophecy historically, we need a revelation of the One about whom Isaiah prophesied. God is with us.

The Son Isaiah prophesied about, God here on earth, has been born, and He is now available to each of us. Jesus is knocking at the door of our hearts. If we open up the door and let Him in, we can experience the full reality of Immanuel.

I want to invite you to participate in a simple exercise as a way of awakening to the presence of God that is with you. Put your hand over your heart and simply say out loud, "God is here. God, You are with me and in me." Do you feel that? That's the witness of the Holy Spirit. He is already here for you.

# CHAPTER 5

# A Multidimensional God

In words that are familiar to many, Jesus tells us in John 3:16 that "God so loved the world, that He gave His only begotten Son, that whoever believes in Him shall not perish, but have eternal life." This foundational text may sound simple to many people, but as a Jewish person, I can tell you the idea that God has a Son is very difficult for us to comprehend.

For centuries, Jewish people have been raised hearing and reciting this declaration from the Torah: "*Sh'ma Yisrael Adonai Eloheinu Adonai Echad.* Hear, O Israel! The LORD is our God, the LORD is one!" This proclamation, called the Shema, is what set Israel apart from all the other nations from the beginning. Found in Deuteronomy 6:4, this pronouncement is the very cornerstone of Jewish belief. Unlike their neighbors, who worshipped many rivaling deities, the people of Israel worshipped only one God. In Judaism, every time we recite the Shema, we re-emphasize this distinction—*that there is only one God.*

The claim, then, that God has a Son seems scandalous to the Jewish mind because it can be interpreted as suggesting there are multiple gods. Using language that refers to God as Father, Son, and Holy Spirit sounds to the conventional Jew like polytheism (the belief in many gods) and raises some questions: Which One? Are you worshipping three gods? Is God divided? This has been a massive source of theological tension between the traditional Jewish community and the Christian community. When someone has been brought up in a traditional Jewish community that emphasizes the oneness of God, the Christian teaching on the Trinity—God as the Father, the Son, and the Holy Spirit—seems to conflict with what they have been taught about God their whole lives.

Yet as we have seen with so many of the revelations of Yeshua in the Hebrew Scriptures, the truth of God's multidimensional nature was embedded there from the start. If we return to the Psalms, which we know were cherished by Yeshua and His early followers, we read these words: "I will surely tell of the decree of the LORD: He said to Me, '*You are My Son, today I have begotten You*'" (Ps. 2:7, emphasis added).

Here we see a glimpse into the Godhead from the New Testament. The language the author of this psalm uses here reminds us of when Yeshua was on the Mount of Transfiguration with His apostles and the voice came from heaven, saying, "This is My beloved Son, with whom I am well-pleased" (Matt. 17:5). Precedence for the mystery of the Trinity or Godhead was already set in the Old Testament. We see this revelation in Psalm 110:1 as well. David writes, "The LORD says to my Lord: 'Sit at My right hand until I make Your enemies a footstool for Your feet.'" Notice David uses the word *Lord* two times in this sentence.

Jesus asked the Pharisees about this very passage, saying in essence, "Who was David speaking of when he said, 'The Lord says to my Lord'?" (See Matthew 22:41–46, a passage we will explore at greater length in chapter 6.) Yeshua was probing the mystery of God's nature that was tucked into the Hebrew Scriptures. David had insight into the revelation that God the Father and His Messiah were of the same essence.

## BEYOND HUMAN LOGIC

How, then, do we understand that God is one—as the Hebrew Scriptures revealed from the beginning—and yet God is Father, Son, and Spirit? This is not an irrational concept; rather, it is a transrational idea—meaning it is beyond our capacity to grasp through reason.

We cannot conceive the fullness of God's nature and how He has always existed by relying on logic alone. Consider this: We can ask, "Where did God come from? How did He get here?" But how do we grasp that God came from nothing? Didn't He have to come from somewhere? How do we comprehend that God is self-existent? It makes no sense to us. The questions are utterly beyond our comprehension. We cannot even come close to grasping by intellectual capacity alone the wonderful, supernatural reality of a loving God who simply *is*—who didn't come from anywhere or anything but has just always existed.

We tend to think in terms of cause and effect, so we want to know where things came from or what caused them to exist. We are told that life began with the big bang, but what caused the big bang? And what caused the thing that caused the big bang?! This line of questioning goes in an infinite circle because we simply do not have the aptitude to think beyond our human categories of cause and effect.

Our finite, human minds cannot apprehend the realm of a self-existent God who came from nowhere but has always been. But the fact is, God is the first cause. Nothing "caused" Him. He has always been. For this same reason, we should not insist on being able to logically understand that God is one and yet within Himself exist a multiplicity of personalities He can display. When we say God is Father, Son, and Holy Spirit, we are not saying there are three gods. Rather, we are saying God is *multidimensional*. There is one God, one essence, and He exists in three persons. He reveals and has manifested Himself as Father, Son, and the Holy Spirit.

Consider again the words of Psalm 2:7, "You are My Son, today I have begotten You." God the Father has a Son who is Himself also God. This amazing revelation of the glory of God is displayed at Yeshua's baptism: "Immediately coming up out of the water, He saw the heavens opening, and the Spirit like a dove descending upon Him; and a voice came out of the heavens: 'You are My beloved Son, in You I am well-pleased'" (Mark 1:10–11). Father God calls Yeshua His Son!

The beauty of this mystery is that within Himself there

is relationship. This is why in the very beginning, the Scriptures say, "Let *Us* make man in *Our* image" (Gen. 1:26, emphasis added). Why do the Hebrew Scriptures use the plural "Us" to speak of God while fiercely maintaining that God is one? Because there is relationship and a multidimensional aspect within the Godhead.

In the bosom of the Father is the Son. He has been forever in the Father and with the Father, and the Father's love is focused on His Son. It is this Son who was made manifest in the world and died for our sin, as the following scriptures attest.

> No one has seen God at any time; *the only begotten God who is in the bosom of the Father,* He has explained Him.
> —JOHN 1:18, EMPHASIS ADDED

> In the beginning was the Word, and the Word was with God, and the Word was God....And the Word became flesh, and dwelt among us, and we saw His glory, glory as of the only begotten from the Father, full of grace and truth.
> —JOHN 1:1, 14

Our human limitations prevent us from fully comprehending the realm of the Spirit. We are the created. The created cannot fully understand his Creator. "'For My thoughts are not your thoughts, nor are your ways My ways,' declares the LORD. 'For as the heavens are higher than the earth, so are My ways higher than your ways and My thoughts than your thoughts'" (Isa. 55:8–9).

## YESHUA THE SON, BORN OF A WOMAN

Another mind-bending reality is that the eternal Son of God would take on flesh and be birthed into the world through a woman (Mary). Being Jewish, I am very cognizant of the fact that traditional Jewish people have no expectation that the Messiah would be divine and think the concept of an eternal God being born into the world through a woman is ridiculous and blasphemous. But God came to the earth through a woman because He wanted to fully unite Himself with the people He wanted to save. The only way He could fully unite Himself with you and me, and enter into the intimacy that He planned to have all along with the human race created in His own image, was to become one of us. And in order to become one of us, He had to come into the world the way you and I did—through a woman.

After Adam and Eve sinned, they needed to be redeemed because their sin separated them from God. They sinned because they tried to get their desires fulfilled outside of God. The serpent came to Eve and said, "Look at this tree. If you eat of it, it's going to make you wise." (See Genesis 3:1–3.) Yet God had said, "From any tree of the garden you may eat freely; but from the tree of the knowledge of good and evil you shall not eat, for in the day that you eat from it you will surely die" (Gen. 2:16–17). Despite God's warning, Eve chose to fulfill her desire outside of God's path for her life. When she saw that the fruit of the tree looked good to her eyes and was told it would make her wise, her desire was aroused.

She ate of the tree. And when she ate of the tree and then gave it to Adam, who also ate of the tree, immediately they realized they were naked—and shame set in.

When shame set in, they hid from God, becoming isolated, afraid, and under the curse of the serpent and death. But after they sinned, God spoke to Adam and Eve and gave them the promise of a coming Messiah in Genesis 3:15: "And I will put enmity between you and the woman, and between your seed and *her seed*; He [Messiah] shall bruise you on the head, and you shall bruise him on the heel" (emphasis added). Notice that this scripture says it would be through the *seed* of the woman that the devil would be crushed. This seed is Yeshua, who was born into the world through a woman to redeem us from Satan's curse, which came upon humanity when Eve fell for Satan's deceptions.

So you see, the promise of our salvation does not begin with the New Testament Gospels; it goes all the way back to Genesis 3:15, which revealed that the Redeemer would come and enter the world through the seed of a woman.

## God Comes to Us in Our Shame

Perhaps you are reading this right now from the same place Adam and Eve found themselves in—a posture of shame. You may have made decisions you are not proud of. You may be all too acquainted, this very moment, with the way shame has stripped you of self-acceptance and caused you to run into darkness, isolation, or addiction.

No matter who you are or what you have done—no matter how dense or heavy the shame that you carry—God has a plan for your life. It is better than anything you can imagine right now. Know that God is not surprised or caught off guard by your sin. He made provision for it long ago and set a plan in motion to pick up, cleanse, and redeem you. Father revealed His means for your redemption in Genesis 3!

You are not an accident. You do not have to be defined by your failures, weaknesses, and mistakes. You are passionately beloved by God the Father, and there is no limit to which He will not go to bring you home to Himself.

Nothing from your past needs to control you or your future. Yet in order to fully step into our destiny, beloved, we need to fully return to our Creator through Messiah Jesus.

In the same way that we cannot fathom God's self-existence or how God is Three yet One, we cannot comprehend why God loves us so relentlessly. He simply does because He chooses to do so.

We have been immersing ourselves in texts that tell us the truth about a multidimensional God and His amazing plan. But these ancient texts are not ancient history. The story of Adam and Eve, including their fall and promise of redemption, is our story. In the same way that God is multidimensional, the Scriptures are multidimensional. As we read of God's activity in the past, we find God bursting into our present, giving us a hopeful future!

As we close this chapter, I want to encourage you to

think about your life. Perhaps there is an area of your life right now where you are struggling with shame. If you are feeling the isolation, alienation, and self-loathing that shame brings, I want to encourage you before you read further to bring that shame into the light of God's presence and ask Yeshua to take that shame away and cleanse you of it. "Everyone who asks receives, and he who seeks finds, and to him who knocks it will be opened" (Matt. 7:8). By His Spirit, by His blood, and by His Word, you and I can be free. Yeshua said, "And you will know the truth, and the truth will make you free.... So if the Son makes you free, you will be free indeed" (John 8:32, 36).

What would it look like right now for you to hand over every bit of your shame to the One who knows everything about you but loves you completely? What could it look like right now to come out of hiding and be fully seen and fully known? In the same way God the Father called Jesus His beloved Son, Father God now calls you His beloved child. When we run into the arms of the Father, there is nothing to hide and nothing left to fear!

# CHAPTER 6

# David—a Type of Messiah

ABRAHAM, ISAAC, AND Jacob are the great patriarchs of the Jewish people—but there is another towering figure that comes later, one who exemplifies and embodies the Hebrew tradition as much as those early figures do: King David. He is one of the great characters in the Hebrew Bible, a man whose life is tied to Israel for all time.

Like Israel, David was once too young, too small, and too unremarkable for anyone to notice him. But also like Israel, we see him slay giants and achieve impossible exploits through God's power. David's story often seems larger than life. It begins with wonder and deep love for God yet also entails him getting it disastrously wrong sometimes. But David would eventually see where he went wrong and turn to the Lord in repentance and humility. He recognized that the presence of God is what set him apart, and he made God's presence central to his life. David would not be a perfect king, but his reign would come to represent Israel at its best and mark its glory years.

We have already seen how the Hebrew Scriptures told us the Messiah would come through the bloodline of Abraham, Isaac, and Jacob. More specifically, though, He was to come through the tribe of Jacob's son Judah as Genesis 49:10 says: "The scepter shall not depart from Judah, nor the ruler's staff from between his feet, until Shiloh [Messiah] comes, and to him shall be the obedience of the peoples." When we follow the trail of Messianic prophecy down through the line of the tribe of Judah, it inevitably leads us to Israel's most celebrated king—David.

It is no coincidence that Yeshua was born in Bethlehem, David's hometown. Bethlehem is still referred to as "the city of David," for it was here that the prophet Samuel anointed David to be king over all of Israel (1 Sam. 16). Some eight centuries before Yeshua was born there, the prophet Micah wrote, "But as for you, Bethlehem Ephrathah, too little to be among the clans of Judah, from you One will go forth for Me to be ruler in Israel. His goings forth are from long ago, from the days of eternity" (Mic. 5:2).

Isaiah, whose name means "God saves," lived approximately seven hundred years before the birth of Yeshua. He received his call during the reign of King Uzziah when the glory of God awesomely and sovereignly fell upon him (Isa. 6). Like Micah, Isaiah prophesied that Messiah would be in the lineage of David and pointed to Messiah's eternal nature.

> For a child will be born to us, a son will be given to us; and the government will rest on His

shoulders; and His name will be called Wonderful Counselor, Mighty God, Eternal Father, Prince of Peace. There will be no end to the increase of His government or of peace, *on the throne of David* and over his kingdom, to establish it and to uphold it with justice and righteousness from then on and forevermore. The zeal of the LORD of hosts will accomplish this.

—ISAIAH 9:6–7, EMPHASIS ADDED

Continuing our journey, we come to the Hebrew prophet Jeremiah, who wrote: "'Behold, days are coming,' declares the LORD, 'when I will fulfill the good word which I have spoken concerning the house of Israel and the house of Judah. [Israel was the name of Israel's northern kingdom, and Judah was the name of Israel's southern kingdom. The northern and southern kingdoms together represented all of Israel's twelve tribes.] In those days and at that time *I will cause a righteous Branch of David to spring forth*; and He shall execute justice and righteousness on the earth'" (Jer. 33:14–15, emphasis added).

Notice how in this scripture Jeremiah revealed that someone from David's line would be called "a righteous Branch of David." We see how Yeshua fulfilled Jeremiah's prophecy for you and me:

But by His doing you are in *Christ Jesus*, who became to us...*righteousness*.

—1 CORINTHIANS 1:30, EMPHASIS ADDED

He made Him who knew no sin to be sin on our behalf, so that we might become the *righteousness of God in Him.*

—2 CORINTHIANS 5:21, EMPHASIS ADDED

## A DAVID YET TO COME

From one prophet of the Hebrew Bible to the next, we see that Messianic prophecy explicitly revealed that Messiah would come into the world through the line of David. One of the clearest passages comes through the prophet Ezekiel: "Therefore, thus says the Lord GOD to them...'Then I will set over them one shepherd, *My servant David*, and he will feed them; he will feed them himself and be their shepherd. And I, the LORD, will be their God, and *My servant David will be prince among them; I the LORD have spoken*'" (Ezek. 34:20, 23–24, emphasis added).

David was long gone by the time the prophet penned these words. In other words, Ezekiel lived after David already died. So who is Ezekiel referring to when he says, "My servant David"? Was Ezekiel claiming that David would be reincarnated to once again rule and reign over the people? No, Ezekiel was not writing about the David who lived four hundred years before Ezekiel wrote his book; he was writing of the Messiah, who identifies Himself as David's offspring. Yeshua said of Himself, "I am the root and the descendant of David, the bright morning star" (Rev. 22:16).

When we revisit the words of Ezekiel through this lens, we can see that Ezekiel was using "David" as a code word for the Messiah. Yeshua came through the blood-line of this ancient king of Israel, identified Himself with him, and took on the fullness of that mantle by becoming Israel's divine king *forever*. Thus, Yeshua said, "I am the root and the descendant of David." So we can now clearly see and understand that Ezekiel's prophecy was referring to a coming descendant of David, who would be the Messiah.

The prophetic mantle of kingship that was on David would ultimately come to fully fall upon Jesus.

The Lord Himself said to David:

> When your days are fulfilled that you must go to be with your fathers, that I will set up one of your descendants after you, who will be of your sons; and I will establish his kingdom. He shall build for Me a house, and I will establish his throne forever. I will be his father and he shall be My son; and I will not take My lovingkindness away from him, as I took it from him who was before you. But I will settle him in My house and in My kingdom forever, and his throne shall be established forever.
>
> —1 CHRONICLES 17:11–14

This prophecy was partially fulfilled by Solomon, David's son, who built the Temple. However, as I have already pointed out, all Messianic prophecies, and this is most certainly one of them, are only truly fulfilled in Yeshua of Nazareth.

Even earlier than Ezekiel, who wrote his book in approximately 592–570 BC, the prophet Isaiah wrote about the Messiah's connection to King David in the eighth century BC.

> For the earth will be full of the knowledge of the LORD as the waters cover the sea. Then in that day the nations will resort to the root of Jesse [who was David's father], who will stand as a signal for the peoples; and His resting place will be glorious.
>
> —ISAIAH 11:9–10

Isaiah's Messianic vision was so clear that he was able to see and prophesy about the character of Messiah and His second coming.

> Then a shoot will spring from the stem of Jesse, and a branch from his roots will bear fruit. The Spirit of the LORD will rest on Him, the spirit of wisdom and understanding, the spirit of counsel and strength, the spirit of knowledge and the fear of the LORD. And He will delight in the fear of the LORD, and He will not judge by what His eyes see, nor make a decision by what His ears hear; but with righteousness He will judge the poor, and decide with fairness for the afflicted of the earth; and He will strike the earth with the rod of His mouth, and with the breath of His lips He will slay the wicked. Also righteousness will be the belt about His loins, and faithfulness the belt about His waist.
>
> And the wolf will dwell with the lamb, and the leopard will lie down with the young goat,

and the calf and the young lion and the fatling together; and a little boy will lead them.

—ISAIAH 11:1–6

Perhaps even more amazingly, it seems that Isaiah prophesied about the second coming of Messiah:

Then it will happen on that day that *the* LORD *will again recover the second time* with His hand the remnant of His people, who will remain, from Assyria, Egypt, Pathros, Cush, Elam, Shinar, Hamath, and from the islands of the sea.

—ISAIAH 11:11, EMPHASIS ADDED

Notice Isaiah's words "the LORD will again recover the second time." In this same eleventh chapter where Isaiah ties the Messiah to Jesse, David's father, he also reveals what life will look like on earth during the Messianic age when God will reign on the earth for a thousand years. (See Revelation 20:1–7.)

And the wolf will dwell with the lamb, and the leopard will lie down with the young goat, and the calf and the young lion and the fatling together; and a little boy will lead them. Also the cow and the bear will graze, their young will lie down together, and the lion will eat straw like the ox. The nursing child will play by the hole of the cobra, and the weaned child will put his hand on the viper's den. They will not hurt or destroy in all My holy mountain, for the earth

will be full of the knowledge of the LORD as the
waters cover the sea.

—ISAIAH 11:6–9

## FROM DAVID TO MARY

Intriguingly, the Gospel of Luke traces the genealogy of
Jesus through David—but with a unique nuance. The
genealogies of Israel, like all ancient genealogies, were
patriarchal; they were traced through the male. In other
words, the identity of a child was determined by the
father. Moses, for example, married a Midianite woman
who was not Hebrew, yet Moses' children were considered Hebrew because he (the father) was a Hebrew.
Throughout the Hebrew Bible we see the identity of a
child consistently being determined through patriarchal
descent. But Luke traces Yeshua's genealogy through
Jesus' mother, Myriam (Mary).

Interestingly, there has been a shift. The rabbinic
courts are no longer basing a child's identity on whether
the child was born to a Jewish father. Now, the mother's lineage determines whether the person is Jewish or
not. There are different theories as to when and why
this shift from patriarchal to matriarchal descent took
place. Both my mother and father are Jewish, so I have
no horse in the race. In my view, someone is Jewish biologically whether his or her father or mother is Jewish.
This is evidently how the Lord sees it because, again,
Luke traces Yeshua's genealogy back to David through
Yeshua's mother, Myriam.

# Yeshua, the Psalms, and
# the New Testament

Notice how David is ever present in Yeshua's use of the psalms. For example, in Matthew 22, Yeshua quotes David's words from Psalm 110:1 in a verbal battle with the Pharisees: "Now while the Pharisees were gathered together, Jesus asked them a question: 'What do you think about the Christ, whose son is He?'" (Matt. 22:41–42). (*Christ* is the Greek word for the Hebrew *Mashiach*, meaning "the Anointed One." Because Greek was the most common language of the world during the time the New Testament was written, the Lord had the New Testament recorded in Greek so He would reach the maximum number of people.)

The Pharisees answered Him, "The son of David" (Matt. 22:42). Yeshua then asked, "Then how does David in the Spirit call Him 'Lord,' saying [from Psalm 110:1], 'The Lord said to my Lord, "Sit at My right hand, until I put Your enemies beneath Your feet"'? If David then calls Him 'Lord,' how is He his son?" (Matt. 22:43–45). Yeshua was blowing their minds! He asked them, "Whose son is the Messiah?" They said, "He's David's son." So Jesus replied to the Pharisees, "How is He David's son if David calls Him his Lord?"

This straightforward question that Yeshua posed brought much confusion and agitation and was unanswerable to the Pharisees. The Bible says they didn't ask Him any more questions after that. As I read how He handled Himself through the entire Brit Chadashah

(New Testament), I am ever amazed at the wisdom and genius of Yeshua! But what we see in Matthew 22 is not just Jesus being quick-witted. Yeshua was revealing Himself through the stories and texts the Jewish people had known and read all along but had not fully understood. In this exchange, He is pointing out that Messiah is physically Lord and from the line of David at the same time. This was a fresh revelation to the religious leaders of Yeshua's day.

**A Psalm of David.**

> The LORD says to my Lord: "Sit at My right
> hand until I make Your enemies a footstool for
> Your feet."
>
> —PSALM 110:1

## YESHUA AS A NEW DAVID

When Jesus came to earth, He looked like a normal human being. There was nothing glamorous about His appearance. It was just like when God commanded the prophet Samuel to go see Jesse because one of his sons was going to be the king. Jesse called his sons, lining them up from the oldest and tallest to the youngest and smallest. Naturally, the prophet started with the oldest, most handsome, most towering son, but he did not feel a witness from the Lord as he stood in front of him. One by one, he went down the line, with nothing stirring in his spirit. Knowing that God told him one of Jesse's sons was going to be king, he was confused. He thought, "Something is not right here." Samuel asked Jesse, "Is there anybody else?"

"Oh, just the little shepherd boy down in the field over there, tending the sheep," Jesse told him. They ran and fetched David, the smallest one. He was the least likely according to the natural eye. But when the prophet laid his hands on David, the Spirit of the Lord bore witness and said, "He's the one." (See 1 Samuel 16:1–13.)

They reacted the same way to Yeshua in Matthew 13:55–57, when the people said, "Is not this the carpenter's son?...And they took offense at Him." In other words, they said, "Who does this guy think He is? We know His mom and dad." Yeshua, like David, was discounted; He didn't look the part of a king.

Can you see that David was a type of Yeshua? As God took David out of obscurity, where he was the smallest, youngest, and least physically impressive of his brothers, and anointed him king, so God anointed Yeshua, a carpenter's son.

Consider also that being despised and rejected was a part of the life David lived. Notice what David said about himself.

> But I am a worm and not a man, a reproach of men and despised by the people. All who see me sneer at me; they separate with the lip, they wag the head, saying, "Commit yourself to the LORD; let Him deliver him; let Him rescue him, because He delights in him." Yet You are He who brought me forth from the womb; You made me trust when upon my

mother's breasts. Upon You I was cast from birth;
You have been my God from my mother's womb.

—PSALM 22:6–10

Compare David's experience to Yeshua's own experience at His crucifixion.

At that time two robbers were crucified with Him,
one on the right and one on the left. And those
passing by were hurling abuse at Him, wagging
their heads and saying, "You who are going to
destroy the temple and rebuild it in three days,
save Yourself! If You are the Son of God, come
down from the cross." In the same way the chief
priests also, along with the scribes and elders,
were mocking Him and saying, "He saved others;
He cannot save Himself. He is the King of Israel;
let Him now come down from the cross, and we
will believe in Him. He trusts in God; let God
rescue Him now, if He delights in Him; for He
said, 'I am the Son of God.'" The robbers who had
been crucified with Him were also insulting Him
with the same words.

—MATTHEW 27:38–44

And Jesus, crying out with a loud voice, said,
"Father, into Your hands I commit My spirit."
Having said this, He breathed His last.

—LUKE 23:46

Can you see the parallel between David and Jesus?
Both were called of God in the most extreme sense yet

experienced utter rejection. Again, this is why Yeshua said in the last chapter of the Bible, Revelation 22, "I am the root and the descendant of David" (v. 16).

Finally, consider that David was called of God to be Israel's king, yet for years he waited on the Lord to bring him into his destiny, refusing to slay King Saul to claim the throne (1 Sam. 24). Likewise, Yeshua, the true King over all creation, refused to call down a legion of angels to slay His enemies (Matt. 26:53–54) but waited upon His Father to exalt Him.

> Being found in appearance as a man, He humbled Himself by becoming obedient to the point of death, even death on a cross. For this reason also, God highly exalted Him, and bestowed on Him the name which is above every name, so that at the name of Jesus every knee will bow, of those who are in heaven and on earth and under the earth, and that every tongue will confess that Jesus Christ is Lord, to the glory of God the Father.
> —PHILIPPIANS 2:8–11

Climactically, as David became Israel's greatest king, so Yeshua became the rightful King of the world.

> Then all the tribes of Israel came to David at Hebron and said, "Behold, we are your bone and your flesh."…So all the elders of Israel came to the king at Hebron, and King David made a covenant with them before the LORD at Hebron; then they anointed David king over Israel.
> —2 SAMUEL 5:1, 3

The prophetic mantle of kingship that was on David would ultimately come to fully fall upon Jesus. I love the scene from heaven the apostle John describes in Revelation 5, where he began to weep because no one was found worthy to open the sacred scroll that would release the end-time events that climax with Yeshua's return.

> And no one in heaven or on the earth or under the earth was able to open the book or to look into it. Then I began to weep greatly because no one was found worthy to open the book or to look into it; and one of the elders said to me, "Stop weeping; behold, the *Lion that is from the tribe of Judah, the Root of David*, has overcome so as to open the book and its seven seals."
> —REVELATION 5:3–5, EMPHASIS ADDED

John later writes:

> Then the seventh angel sounded; and there were loud voices in heaven, saying, "The kingdom of the world has become the kingdom of our Lord and of His Christ; and He will reign forever and ever."
> —REVELATION 11:15

Yeshua was faithful in the face of every temptation, trial, and failure, even unto death. David's reign ended when he went to the grave, but this new descendant of David conquered something far greater than a giant—he conquered death itself, overcoming it with His resurrection so that, as the angel proclaimed, His rule and reign will have no end (Luke 1:32–33)!

## FROM DAVID TO JESUS TO YOU

Our mission on the earth right now is to seek and know Him so we can be transformed into His likeness and boldly proclaim His truth. We are called to be His bold witnesses to the world.

The exploits of King David in Scripture are great, but they only anticipated an even greater fulfillment. Seeing the clear ways the story of Israel's greatest king finds its climax in Yeshua should give us confidence and clarity in witnessing for Him. The world cannot afford for us to be timid and unclear.

You may be experiencing pressure to play down your witness of Yeshua. If you feel that pressure, know that you are not alone—there is a great cloud of witnesses that have gone before you. As Yeshua connected His life and ministry to the prophetic tradition that came before Him, so too He told us that those who came after Him would experience rejection as He and the prophets of old did. Yes, it is painful to experience marginalization because of our witness. But know that facing resistance is nothing new.

That is my prayer as you are reading this now—that the same Spirit who anointed the words of Ezekiel, raised up David, and climactically raised Yeshua from the dead would breathe grace, strength, and courage into you and me. Beloved, Yeshua stands with you. He said, "Peace be with you; as the Father has sent Me, I also send you" (John 20:21). We are surrounded by a great cloud of witnesses who throughout the ages have faithfully borne witness of Him. So, "go into all the world and preach the gospel to all creation. He who has believed and has been baptized shall be saved; but he who has disbelieved shall be condemned" (Mark 16:15–16).

CHAPTER 7

# Messiah's Birth Revealed in the Old Testament

ALTHOUGH WE TOUCHED upon this in chapter 4, I want to look with you more fully at how Yeshua's birth is a foundational fulfillment of Messianic prophecy. The Hebrew Scriptures reveal that the concept of supernatural birth was in place long before Jesus arrived in flesh and bone, preparing us for what was to come.

You likely know the story of how Yeshua was birthed into the world: An angel appeared to Myriam (Mary), Jesus' mother, to tell her she had conceived by the Ruach HaKodesh, the very breath of God. When Joseph, to whom she was engaged, heard Mary was bearing a child, he was thinking of putting her away because culturally it was a terribly shameful thing for her to have become pregnant before they were married.

The angel, however, convinced Joseph that this conception was supernatural and of God, so Joseph proceeded to marry her. But the child Joseph and Myriam raised was no ordinary boy. Again, He didn't come through natural means. It wasn't Joseph's sperm that led to the child being born into the world. Rather, Yeshua was born as a result of a miraculous impregnation.

Jesus' supernatural birth narrative is sometimes dismissed as a mere myth. But as we saw in chapter 4, the story of the Hebrew people already hung on the concept of supernatural birth, going back to Avraham (Abraham), the father of us all.

When God told Abraham in Genesis 18 that he was going to bear a child through his wife, Sarah, Abraham was already long past hope of childbearing. Sarah famously laughed at the absurdity of the idea that she would still conceive at ninety years old. But God rebuked her and told both Abraham and Sarah they would have the child they so greatly desired but had given up on, saying in verse 14, "Is anything too difficult for the LORD? At the appointed time I will return to you, at this time next year, and Sarah will have a son."

They surely could not have imagined then just how much their lives really could change in a year—how concrete, real, and alive this promise would feel when they actually held their little son in their arms. God is always faithful to do what He says He's going to do, and sure enough, a year later, when Abraham was a hundred years old, Sarah gave birth to Isaac. Isaac's birth carried on a lineage that began with Abraham and would continue with Isaac's son Jacob and extend all the way down to Yeshua Himself. As it was with Sarah, the God of resurrection invaded Myriam's life with a promise beyond comprehension. She would give birth to the Son of God despite the fact that she had never had sexual relations with a man.

It was God who supernaturally gave life to Abraham's and Sarah's organs to bring forth Isaac. And it was the Ruach HaKodesh who came upon Mary and overshadowed her with His creative power to birth Yeshua into the world supernaturally. Israel's story began with a supernatural birth through Sarah, a woman who was too old to conceive, and it culminated with a supernatural birth by a woman, Mary (Myriam), who had never known a man. *Nothing* is too hard for the Lord!

Notice here how Yeshua's supernatural birth fills Israel's history up with meaning. Israel was acquainted with the supernatural birth of Abraham's son Isaac through his ninety-year-old wife. But Yeshua's supernatural birth through a virgin takes the concept to a whole new level. And why wouldn't the Son of God's birth into the world be the most spectacularly supernatural one of all? He is the Central One, the most unique being to ever enter our planet. He is God made flesh, the Father's gift to humanity.

## THE ONE FROM BETHLEHEM, ROOTED IN ETERNITY

In his Gospel, Matthew amplifies the words of the prophet Isaiah when he says, "'Behold, the virgin shall be with child and shall bear a Son, and they shall call His name Immanuel,' which translated means, 'God with us'" (Matt. 1:23; see also Isaiah 7:14). Matthew's

Gospel aims to show us how the Law of Moses, the Prophets, and the Psalms—the Hebrew Bible—all point to and find their ultimate purpose in Yeshua.

Moving on from the way Messiah was born to where He was born, consider that the Hebrew prophet Micah specifically tells us the Messiah would come from Bethlehem! "But as for you, *Bethlehem* Ephrathah, too little to be among the clans of Judah, from you One will go forth for Me to be ruler in Israel. His goings forth are from long ago, from the days of eternity" (Mic. 5:2, emphasis added).

We read of this prophecy's fulfillment in Matthew 2:1–6, when King Herod asked the chief priests and scribes where the Messiah was to be born, and they told him, "In *Bethlehem* of Judea; for this is what has been written by the prophet: 'And you, Bethlehem, land of Judah, are by no means least among the leaders of Judah; for out of you shall come forth a Ruler who will shepherd My people Israel'" (vv. 5–6, emphasis added). As Micah predicted, the One from tiny Bethlehem is going to be the ruler of the nations; One from eternity will be coming into the world. It almost seems like a myth, like it's too wonderful to be true, but it is. The One who will come out of Bethlehem will be rooted in eternity.

You should know that in traditional Judaism, the expectation is for a Messiah who will just be a man. In fact, traditional Judaism teaches that there is a potential Messiah in every generation. They believe the Messiah will do great things, that He will turn the people of Israel back to faithful observance of the Torah. Of course, the difference is that as believers in

Yeshua, our understanding is that the Messiah is more than just a great man—He is, rather, God Himself clothed in humanity.

This is what Micah the Hebrew prophet clarifies—that this Messiah who will begin His work from Bethlehem is "from the days of eternity." The prophet Isaiah, too, saw that Messiah would be eternal in nature, as we read in Isaiah 9:6: "For a child will be born to us, a son will be given to us; and the government will rest on His shoulders; and His name will be called Wonderful Counselor, Mighty God, *Eternal* Father, Prince of Peace" (emphasis added).

The Gospel of John in particular highlights how Yeshua fulfills this prophecy, underscoring that He is not only the Jewish Messiah but the eternal One. As seen earlier, John 1:1, 14 tells us, "In the beginning was the Word, and the Word was with God, and the Word was God....And the Word became flesh, and dwelt among us, and we saw His glory, glory as of the only begotten from the Father, full of grace and truth." In John 8:58, Yeshua says directly of Himself, "Truly, truly, I say to you, before Abraham was born, I am."

## ROOTED IN THE WORD

Matthew roots his telling of the birth of Yeshua in the promise made in Micah 5:2, not in a fairy tale, which is what many churchgoers silently believe. This is why having deep roots in the Hebrew Scriptures matters: it strengthens us. In this age when it is not politically correct to believe in and proclaim the exclusivity of Christ Jesus, without a good grasp of how our faith in Messiah is rooted in the whole Word, we are going to be like a branch that is tossed back and forth in the wind. Like a boat on the sea without a rudder, we will be blown whichever way the culture bends. Understanding how our faith in Jesus is rooted in the Tanakh anchors us.

It is a lack of grounding in the Word that causes people to bow to political correctness instead of becoming bold witnesses. People will tell us it is not necessary to share our faith, that it infringes on other people's beliefs. But that kind of faith is not apostolic. My hope, beloved one, is that by seeing how Jesus fulfills the Messianic prophecy of the Old Testament, your spine will be strengthened, you will have peace, and you will be His witness.

## ALL THINGS ARE POSSIBLE

Because you are in relationship with the God who supernaturally gave a child to Abraham and Sarah, your life is not a dead end, no matter what circumstances you are in. The situation you are facing may look impossible to you, but it is certainly not impossible to God. As you root yourself in the truth of these Hebrew stories, my prayer is that you will allow this hope to take root in you!

Once again, I want to invite you to take inventory of anything in your life that seems impossible. Like Abraham and Sarah, you have looked at "the facts" and know there is nothing you could do to make anything happen. Perhaps for you, as it was for Sarah, the idea of seeing anything change at this point seems so absurd it is just laughable.

Maybe it is not even so much that you question God, but you question yourself. Like Sarah, you know your mortal limits, and you have resigned yourself to a particular fate. You may think you are just too old now, or this has gone on this way for too long, or it is just too late. You have looked at your circumstance from every possible angle and cannot imagine a solution. You feel stuck—like there is no way out and that nothing new or creative could happen.

Sometimes we see our lives this way, and naturally speaking, we are not wrong. The situation may actually *not* be possible for us to change. But Yeshua said in Matthew 19:26 (KJV), "With men this is impossible; but with God all things are possible." As you are thinking about that situation that is unsolvable to you, why not take a moment right now and intentionally hand it over to the God of Avraham? Give Him what you have given up on. If the God we worship gave a son to Abraham and Sarah in their old age, do you really not believe He can still surprise you? Sometimes it is not the physical situation that will change but our perception of it. This may revolutionize everything. Hear the question one more time spoken into you over and over: "Is anything too difficult for the Lord?"

# CHAPTER 8

# Unwavering Faith

HUNDREDS OF YEARS before the birth of Yeshua, Jewish people believed Elijah, the messenger of God, would come and prepare the way for the Messiah's coming. Malachi 3:1 says, "'Behold, I am going to send My messenger, and he will clear the way before Me. And the Lord, whom you seek, will suddenly come to His temple; and the messenger of the covenant, in whom you delight, behold, He is coming,' says the LORD of hosts." The prophet goes further in Malachi 4:5, saying, "Behold, I am going to send you Elijah the prophet before the coming of the great and terrible day of the LORD." The prophecy was that before Messiah would appear in the earth, Elijah the Hebrew prophet would appear first to clear space for Him and prepare the world for His coming.

If you have ever experienced the Passover meal called the *seder*, you know how prominent a place this specific prophecy has in Jewish tradition. Whenever the Passover seder is celebrated, we set a place at the table that is left empty—a place that sits unoccupied for Elijah. In addition to reserving a chair and cup for Elijah, we have a child run to the door of the house or building where we are holding the Passover seder meal to look outside to see if Elijah is coming. It is symbolic of inviting Elijah to come back so he can announce that Messiah is here.

We do these things at Passover because we believe that even as the Lord delivered the Israelites out of Egypt thirty-five hundred years ago, He is going to deliver the children of Israel again when the Messiah arrives, preceded by Elijah.

You can understand, then, why when Yeshua came, people were asking, "If You're the Messiah, where is Elijah? Why hasn't he come?" Those who did not believe were saying Jesus could not be the Messiah since apparently Elijah had not yet appeared to announce Him. Yeshua responded by saying Elijah had, in fact, already visited them, if they were willing to accept it, in the person of John (Yohanan) the Baptist.

Consider Yeshua's words:

> If you are willing to accept it, John himself is Elijah who was to come.
>
> —MATTHEW 11:14

> And His disciples asked Him, "Why then do the scribes say that Elijah must come first?" And He answered and said, "Elijah is coming and will restore all things; but I say to you that Elijah already came, and they did not recognize him, but did to him whatever they wished. So also the Son

of Man is going to suffer at their hands." Then the disciples understood that He had spoken to them about John the Baptist.

—MATTHEW 17:10–13

This helps us to appreciate more fully John the Baptist's words recorded in the Gospel of John 1:23: "I am a voice of one crying in the wilderness, 'Make straight the way of the Lord.'" His words brought Isaiah's prophecy to a whole new level, establishing it in fulfillment: "A voice is calling, 'Clear the way for the LORD in the wilderness; make smooth in the desert a highway for our God'" (Isa. 40:3).

## THE TRUTH HIDDEN IN PLAIN SIGHT

Sometimes the truth is hidden in plain sight, right in front of our eyes, eager to be discovered. Sadly, both in Jesus' time and in our own, many religious Jews who have the most direct access to the truth of the ancient Scriptures often choose not to believe. Few of my people have recognized that Yeshua is the Messiah.

To give you some insight into how strong of an anti-Jesus mindset exists within the traditional Jewish community, consider that as soon as I received Jesus as Messiah in 1978 at the age of twenty—more than forty years ago now—I was disqualified by my people from even being considered a Jew anymore. (For my complete story, please get my autobiography, *Called to Breakthrough*.)

Unfortunately, even within the church there are those who look at me and other Jews like me—those of us who have received Jesus as the Messiah—as somehow no longer being authentically Jewish. But if Jesus really is the Jewish Messiah and I have received Him as a Jew, how can someone look at me and tell me I am not authentically Jewish anymore because I believe Jesus is Messiah? Do you have to *not* believe in Jesus to be authentically Jewish? Consider that He died on the cross with a sign over His head that said, "Yeshua of Nazareth, King of the Jews." (See John 19:19.) If He really is the King of the Jews, how can people like me be considered no longer Jewish by Jews and Gentiles alike for believing in Him?

As someone who was born a Jew, came into the world through two Jewish parents, and was raised as a Jew and bar mitzvahed in a conservative synagogue—I am Jewish. In fact, my Ancestry.com results show that I am 100 percent Jewish. I have grown out my peyos (side curls) to make a visible statement that you can be fully Jewish and believe that Jesus is the Messiah. For me, believing in Jesus is the most Jewish thing I can do.

## THE CALL TO LET GO

I am aware that most people who follow my ministry, Discovering the Jewish Jesus (www.discoveringthejewishjesus.com), do not share my Jewish experience. While believing in Jesus as Messiah has come at a cost, I do not share my story to be heroic. I share it because whoever you are and wherever you are, I want to encourage you to be bold in your faith and witness.

One of the things that has shifted in our culture is

that there is no longer an agreed-upon set of values or truth. Today, people can get online and propagate anything at all—and if it is said long enough, people will often begin to believe it is truth. You have probably heard the saying, "If a lie is repeated enough, eventually people lose sight of the fact that it's a lie and begin to accept it as truth." We are living in a society that makes it increasingly difficult to discern what the truth is, and many lies have been accepted hook, line, and sinker.

We are constantly told that there is no such thing as objective truth, that all truth is subjective—simply a matter of perspective or opinion, with no person's truth being higher or better than anyone else's. What we call truth is constantly shifting and evolving as the world modernizes, depending on what trends and currents prevail in popular culture. The answers seem to be always changing. Too often we do whatever the dominant culture is doing at the time.

My wife and thirty-year-old daughter were just talking about how when my daughter was a baby, the doctors told my wife that our daughter should be laid down to sleep on her stomach, that it was unsafe for a baby to sleep on her back. Now that my daughter has infants, the doctors are telling her the opposite. The judgments and opinions of the broader culture, sometimes even inside religious communities, are blatantly unreliable.

God's Word, however, does not shift and change with the times. God's Word is the same yesterday, today, and forever. (See Hebrews 13:8.) Messianic prophecy grounds us in the truth of God's Word. Rooted, established truth does not come and go with the trends of the current moment.

Our technology is new, but the question "What is truth?" is not. The question goes back thousands of years to when Yeshua stood before Pilate, saying, "I have come into the world, to testify to the truth." Pilate responded, "What is truth?" (John 18:37–38).

I want to call you back to the Word. Being grounded in the Word leads us to know that the world is not our standard or compass. Just because the world says something is OK, that does not make it right. As you are seeing how Yeshua fulfilled Old Testament prophecies, solidifying your faith in the authenticity of the Word of God, I want you now to take this confidence in God's Word and apply His Word to everything in your life. Our ultimate question must always be, What does God's Word say about this matter?

For each of us, submitting to God and the authority of His Word is going to cost us. This is why Yeshua said, "If anyone wishes to come after Me, he must deny himself, and take up his cross daily and follow Me" (Luke 9:23), and, "Whoever wishes to save his life will lose it, but whoever loses his life for My sake and the gospel's will save it" (Mark 8:35). Each of us must daily be asking the Lord what He wants us to think and do.

The rich young ruler said to Jesus, "'Good Teacher, what shall I do to inherit eternal life?'…Looking at him, Jesus felt a love for him and said to him, 'One thing you lack: go and sell all you possess and give to the poor, and you will have treasure in heaven; and come, follow

Me'" (Mark 10:17, 21). The rich man walked away sorrowful—he was grieved. He couldn't do it. The point is, truly following Jesus costs us something. It means dying to our own agendas. We must submit to His lordship and, like our Master, say, "Not my will, but Yours be done." (See Luke 22:42.)

Whatever you are clinging to for your confidence, whatever you are clinging to for your security, whatever you are clinging to for your identity, whatever you are clinging to in life other than Him—you have to let go. Yeshua was saying to the rich young man and to you and me, "Unless you give up your false securities and trust Me, you will not be able to fully enter into the experience and reality of eternal life."

If we believe Yeshua fulfilled the Messianic prophecies, our response should not be to merely rejoice that we understand how the Old and New Testament Scriptures fit together. This is not enough. Instead, you and I need to take upon our lives the same challenge He gave to the rich young man: we need to let go of everything and become a fully submitted follower of His. This is what is required of a true disciple of Jesus. We are not learning for the sake of information; we are receiving His summons to *let go*.

## LOOKING FOR GOD

We began this chapter by talking about how most Jewish people missed their Messiah when He first came two thousand years ago. As a result, Jewish people continue to set a chair for Elijah each year at Passover hoping their Messiah will come. My point is that Messiah has come, but as Isaiah prophesied, He was not recognized when He did (Isa. 53). As you think about this, I want you to ask yourself, "What ways might God be revealing Himself to me now that I simply have not realized?" Sometimes we pray for miracles when really what we need is the miracle of sight, of recognition, to see the ways God is working in our lives right now and see that He has already come.

To put it another way, when Yeshua came, He came in a form most of His own people did not recognize or expect. What prayers have you been praying that God is already answering right now, only in a form you are not discerning? Is it possible that you are asking God to speak but have not been able to perceive how He already is speaking? Could you be asking God to move and yet you have not had eyes to see the ways in which He is already moving in your life? For hundreds of years, Jewish people longed and waited for the appearance of the Messiah, but when Messiah came, they could not see Him for who He was.

Do you want to recognize the ways Yeshua has been walking with you in a form that you may not have recognized, as happened to those disciples on the road to Emmaus (Luke 24:13–27)? Yeshua is not hiding; He is here, walking alongside you, present and eager to be found. "Ask, and it will be given to you; seek, and you will find; knock, and it will be opened to you" (Matt. 7:7).

CHAPTER 9

# The Rejected Messiah

THE BOOK OF Isaiah contains some of the strongest prophecy about the Messiah in the Hebrew Bible. Isaiah's prophecies have already been central in our study, but now I want to look closely at Isaiah chapter 53, as it describes the rejection, contempt, and suffering Messiah would have to endure in order to bring healing and salvation to the world. Indeed, this chapter in the Tanakh is both foundational as well as a summit point of Messianic prophecy.

Keep in mind that the very concept of chapters and verses in the Bible did not exist when Isaiah's words were first written down on scrolls. The Bible was divided into chapters in approximately AD 1227 and into verses around 1448. The first entire Bible divided by chapter and verse was published in approximately 1555.[1] Today, we are able to easily refer to texts by chapters and verses, but when the scroll of Isaiah was first written, there were no chapter divisions. It was all one scroll. He did not write Isaiah 52, decide it was complete, and then move on to chapter 53.

There is a funny Jewish story of a person who was standing in the synagogue reading the Torah portion for the day from the Torah scroll and lost his place. (In synagogues, the Torah is still read in scroll form with no chapters or verses.) He said, "I lost my place, and there are no markings in this Torah scroll." A person a little bit off to the side said, "You were reading from the place where it says, 'The Lord said to Moses.'" The joke is that when you read through the Torah, the phrase "the Lord said to Moses" occurs over and over again. You could not find your place by locating the spot that says, "The Lord said to Moses."

But since we are now the beneficiaries of easy-to-reference chapters and verses that translators added to help readers easily find their place, I can walk you verse by verse through several of the Messianic prophecies found in Isaiah 53.

Who has believed our message? And to whom has the arm of the LORD been revealed? For He grew up before Him like a tender shoot, and like a root out of parched ground; He has no stately form or majesty that we should look upon Him, nor appearance that we should be attracted to Him. He was despised and forsaken of men, a man of sorrows and acquainted with grief; and like one from whom men hide their face He was despised, and we did not esteem Him.

Surely our griefs He Himself bore, and our sorrows He carried; yet we ourselves esteemed Him stricken, smitten of God, and afflicted. But He was pierced through for our transgressions, He was crushed for our iniquities; the chastening for our well-being fell upon Him, and by His scourging we are healed. All of us like sheep have gone astray, each of us has turned to his own way; but the LORD has caused the iniquity of us all to fall on Him.

He was oppressed and He was afflicted, yet He did not open His mouth; like a lamb that is led to slaughter, and like a sheep that is silent before its shearers, so He did not open His mouth. By oppression and judgment He was taken away; and as for His generation, who considered that He was cut off out of the land of the living for the transgression of my people, to whom the stroke was due? His grave was assigned with wicked men, yet He was with a rich man in His death, because He had done no violence, nor was there any deceit in His mouth.

But the LORD was pleased to crush Him, putting Him to grief; if He would render Himself as a guilt offering, He will see His offspring, He will prolong His days, and the good pleasure of the LORD will prosper in His hand. As a result of the anguish of His soul, He will see it and be satisfied; by His knowledge the Righteous One, My Servant, will justify the many, as He will bear their iniquities. Therefore, I will allot Him a portion with the great, and He will divide the booty with the strong; because He poured out Himself to death, and was numbered with the transgressors; yet He Himself bore the sin of many, and interceded for the transgressors.

—ISAIAH 53:1–12

Let's begin with verse 1. The prophet asks, "Who has believed our message? And to whom has the arm of the LORD been revealed?" In other words, he's asking, "Who would ever believe this?" Messiah and His message are not going to be believed. The Messiah wasn't going to show up and grow up in some spectacular way that would draw everyone's attention. Rather, Isaiah writes, "He grew up before Him like a tender shoot, and like a root out of parched ground; He has no stately form or majesty that we should look upon Him" (v. 2). Nothing about His physical form was attractive or remarkable. According to the standards of the world, Messiah simply did not look like much. Nothing about Him stood out. He appeared quite average and normal.

While the New Testament is filled with powerful accounts of Yeshua speaking to crowds and performing miracles, and the results of Yeshua's healing touch may have been conspicuous to those who needed and wanted it, He Himself was apparently inconspicuous. He didn't walk into a room with such undeniable charisma or dazzling looks that people automatically thought, "He *has* to be the one we were looking for." Whether it was the religious leaders or the crowds of onlookers, many simply didn't know what to do with Yeshua precisely because they didn't think He looked the part.

Not only was Yeshua overlooked because He did not stand out in appearance or stature as someone of significance; Isaiah goes on to say He was even "despised and rejected by men" (v. 3, NKJV). One of the primary reasons Yeshua was despised and rejected in Israel at

His first coming was because He was outside the box of religious norms. The Pharisees had developed a very legalistic religious system that Yeshua largely dismissed.

For example, in Mark 7, Jesus got in a clash with the Pharisees because His disciples were not washing their hands before eating bread, which was the custom of the Pharisees. Angrily, the Pharisees challenged Yeshua as to why His disciples were not respecting the "tradition of the elders" (v. 5). Yeshua's response to them was that they (the Pharisees) had replaced the true Word of God with their own man-made, religious traditions. Interestingly, Yeshua quoted Isaiah in His reply to these religious leaders:

> And He said to them, "Rightly did Isaiah prophesy of you hypocrites, as it is written: 'This people honors Me with their lips, but their heart is far away from Me. But in vain do they worship Me, teaching as doctrines the precepts of men.' Neglecting the commandment of God, you hold to the tradition of men."
>
> —MATTHEW 7:6–8

Not only did Jesus do things differently and explain God's Word differently from the Pharisees of His day, but on top of that, He pointed His finger at His contemporary religious leaders and called them hypocrites. You see, Jesus was a revolutionary. He was a pioneer, and the first one through the wall always gets bloody. He was the odd man out. So you can imagine why He was rejected.

In fact, the religious leaders became so threatened by Him that they plotted to kill Him (Matt. 26:4; John 11:53).

It reminds me of an old-time Mafia war where a Mafia family controlled a territory, and if a member of another Mafia family tried to do business in that territory, the family in control would put out a hit on the person who was invading its territory. That is essentially what was going on. Yeshua walked into the territory of the Pharisees, who were the religious leaders of His day, and thousands upon thousands who had been following the Pharisees were now turning away from them to follow Yeshua.

You have to understand that in the days when the New Testament was written, the religious leaders were the leaders of society. The religious leaders enjoyed the privilege and power of living at the top of the social spectrum. They were the elite of the day, and they had influence over the masses. The religious leaders fiercely rejected Yeshua because He exposed them as hypocrites, and then they turned the masses against Him. Consider this: Just before Jesus was about to be crucified, Pilate asked the Jewish crowd, "'Whom do you want me to release for you? Barabbas, or Jesus who is called Christ?' For he knew that because of envy they had handed Him over." And "the chief priests and the elders persuaded the crowds to ask for Barabbas and to put Jesus to death" (Matt. 27:17–18, 20).

The powers of darkness focused all their energy on the elimination of the One who had come into the darkness in order that men might see the light. The darkness hates the light and cannot stop itself from doing so.

Of course, Isaiah foresaw that the Messiah would be rejected, but the idea of the Messiah being rejected by Israel, although clearly seen by Isaiah, largely escaped the religious leadership of Yeshua's day. They were not looking for a Messiah who would be rejected. They were looking for someone who would be king. Isaiah clearly saw that the Messiah would suffer and die, but the religious leaders were not looking for a Messiah who would suffer; they were looking for someone who would lead the Jewish nation into freedom and reign in Israel.

I should note that there is a concept in religious Judaism that the Messiah may come as what is called Mashiach ben Yossef, or Messiah, son of Joseph—a Messiah who would be rejected and suffer at the hands of his brothers just like Joseph did (Gen. 37). But the majority of the people were looking for Mashiach ben David, a Messiah who would come from the line of David and restore Israel to glory. Because the religious establishment of Yeshua's day was not looking for Messiah ben Yossef but Messiah ben David, they missed Him. In fact, Paul says "for until this very day" there is a veil over the Jewish people's hearts keeping them from recognizing Yeshua, the suffering servant, as Israel's Messiah (2 Cor. 3:14–15; Rom. 11:25).

Even today some in Israel refer to Him not as Yeshua but as Yeshu, a play on His correct name that is an acronym meaning "May His name be blotted out." Yeshua is seen as someone who betrayed His Jewish faith.

I want to point out here, however, once again that the day is coming when the Jewish people and the nation of

Israel will see Yeshua for who He is—the Savior of the world and the Messiah of Israel.

> For I do not want you, brethren, to be uninformed of this mystery—so that you will not be wise in your own estimation—that a partial hardening has happened to Israel until the fullness of the Gentiles has come in; and so all Israel will be saved; just as it is written, "The Deliverer will come from Zion, He will remove ungodliness from Jacob. This is My covenant with them when I take away their sins."
>
> —ROMANS 11:25–27

Continuing in Isaiah 53, verse 4 says, "Surely our griefs He Himself bore." The Hebrew word translated as "griefs" in this verse is *choli*, and it means sickness and disease.[2] Now I want you to consider this in light of what happened when Jesus came down from the mountain from which He preached His longest sermon in the Bible, which we call the Sermon on the Mount.

As Jesus makes His way down the mountain, He begins to heal. First He heals a leper (Matt. 8:2); then He heals a man who is paralyzed (Matt. 8:6–13). Next Yeshua heals Peter's mother-in-law, and the story climaxes with these words: "When evening came, they brought to Him many who were demon-possessed; and He cast out the spirits with a word, and healed all who were ill. This was to fulfill what was spoken through Isaiah the prophet: 'He Himself took our infirmities and carried away our diseases'" (Matt. 8:16–17).

What I want you to get here is that Matthew's explanation for Jesus' healing all who were ill was in fulfillment of Isaiah's words in Isaiah 53:4, "Our griefs [sicknesses] He Himself bore." What I find so phenomenal about this is that we see here that physical healing is rooted and has its foundation in the atonement. Isaiah 53 is foundationally about Yeshua dying in our place so we can be forgiven and saved. In the New Testament, which was originally written in Greek, the word for *saved* is *sozo*, and the same word is used throughout the Gospels to apply to forgiveness of our sins, the healing of our bodies, and deliverance from tormenting demons.

> She will bear a Son; and you shall call His name Jesus, for He will save [sozo] His people from their sins.
>
> —MATTHEW 1:21

> And behold, one of the rulers of the synagogue came, Jairus by name. And when he saw Him, he fell at His feet and begged Him earnestly, saying, "My little daughter lies at the point of death. Come and lay Your hands on her, that she may be healed [sozo], and she will live."
>
> —MARK 5:22–23, NKJV

> Those who had seen it reported to them how the man who was demon-possessed had been made well [sozo].
>
> —LUKE 8:36

Notice in each of these incidents—from being saved from sin (Matt. 1:21) to being physically healed (Mark 5:23) to being delivered from evil spirits (Luke 8:36)—the same word *sozo* is being used. Many times we can trust Jesus to forgive us of our sins and take us to heaven, but we have a hard time trusting Him to keep our physical bodies healthy or take care of us in the here and now. But the same chapter in Isaiah that speaks about Jesus being pierced through for our transgressions also speaks about Him taking upon Himself our sickness and infirmities, and this is why Matthew points to Isaiah 53:4 as the explanation for the healings Jesus was performing.

Isaiah continues by revealing that Yeshua "carried our sorrows" (Isa. 53:4, NKJV). I want you to get this. The Hebrew word translated "sorrows" in this verse is *makob*, and it refers to emotional suffering and pain.[3] The point is that Jesus our Messiah is a complete Savior. We can cast our entire life upon Him. We can trust Him to take us to heaven, but we can also trust Him for health, physical healing, *and the healing of our emotional and psychic pain right now.*

Certain sectors of the church have put much emphasis on Yeshua as our physical healer, but oftentimes seeing Jesus as our emotional healer has not been emphasized. Some of the most moving moments in my ministry have been when I have seen Yeshua bring emotional healing to His people. The types of encounters I have witnessed cannot be faked. As I have released emotional healing through Yeshua, He has made Himself known and felt. Countless times I have witnessed tears streaming down the faces of those He was healing as they were being set free. He truly has fulfilled and is fulfilling Isaiah's prophecy today, and He will continue to bind up the brokenhearted. Yeshua was wounded for our healing—spirit, soul, and body. He is our healer.

Isaiah explains that Yeshua was not crucified as a punishment for His own transgressions but that He willingly took on the punishment for ours: "He was pierced through for our transgressions, He was crushed for our iniquities; the chastening for our well-being fell upon Him, and by His scourging we are healed" (Isa. 53:5). As previously discussed, the Torah, through the Levitical sacrificial system, and the Tanakh, particularly Isaiah 53, teach the concept of *substitutionary, sacrificial atonement*, whereby we see that the innocent can atone for the guilty by the giving of their own life. This is what Yeshua did.

Again, this concept that Isaiah describes is not novel. It had already been established in the Torah and in Judaic thought that a righteous man could die in the place of the guilty, thereby releasing the guilty from his debt. As mentioned earlier, this is why Caiaphas the high priest said to the religious leaders in relation to Yeshua's impending death, "'It is expedient for you that one man die for the people, and that the whole nation not perish.' Now he did not say this on his own initiative, but being high priest that year, he prophesied that Jesus was going to die for the nation" (John 11:50–51).

Second Corinthians 5:21 says of Yeshua, "He made Him who knew no sin to be sin on our behalf, so that we might become the righteousness of God in Him." Jesus endured the shame and torment of the cross not because He deserved it, but because He loved us enough to pay the ultimate price to make us whole. Everything He suffered was for our healing. Peter references this in the New Testament, saying, "By His wounds you were healed" (1 Pet. 2:24).

Isaiah continues, "All of us like sheep have gone astray, each of us has turned to his own way; but the LORD has caused the iniquity of us all to fall on Him" (Isa. 53:6). We all have chosen to go our own way at times. Yet even while knowing all the ways we would turn from Him, Yeshua died for us.

There are people today who antagonistically claim they don't need Jesus to die for them. This reminds me of a sad incident I witnessed in Colorado several years ago. I was hiking up a mountain to go fishing when I passed a man on the left side of the road who had set up a mini-trailer and was sitting outside of it on a lawn chair. I felt led to reach out to him because he looked really beaten down. I spent a minute or so talking to him and then continued up the mountain to the lake. A few hours later, as I was hiking back down the mountain, I passed him again and felt led to share the gospel with him. He looked at me with hatred and vile darkness in his eyes and said, "I'd rather burn in hell than have Jesus die for my sins." I felt a deep remorse and the powers of hell as I imagined what this man's end was going to be.

Incredibly and regally, Yeshua sacrificed His life without maintaining His innocence or railing against the injustice being done to Him. Isaiah 53:7 says, "He was oppressed and He was afflicted, yet He did not open His mouth; like a lamb that is led to slaughter, and like a sheep that is silent before its shearers, so He did not open His mouth." Standing before Pilate about to be crucified, Jesus did not object. He did not shout. He did not protest, "But I'm innocent!" Rather, He stood there in silence, just like the prophet Isaiah said He would. He did not defend Himself.

This really shook Pilate to the core—to see Jesus standing before him with such a calmness, such a peace, such a confidence, such internal power and an inward self-possession in the eternal Holy Spirit. As authorities often do when they are afraid of losing control, Pilate tried to flex his power instead of admitting how terrified he was. You can almost hear the tremble in his voice when he demands, "Do You not know that I have authority to release You, and I have authority to crucify You?" (John 19:10). In response, Jesus calmly said, "You would have no authority over Me, unless it had been given you from above" (John 19:11). Yeshua willingly offered Himself as a "lamb...to slaughter" (Isa. 53:7). Just as Isaiah predicted, He didn't say a word on His own behalf.

Isaiah goes on to say, "By oppression and judgment He was taken away; *and as for His generation, who considered* that He was cut off out of the land of the living for the transgression of my people, to whom the stroke was due?" (Isa. 53:8, emphasis added). In other words, no one really thought anything about Yeshua once He was crucified. Life went on. People went on about their routines as if nothing had happened. Even though He endured judgment with unprecedented grace, humility, strength, and a fierce love of God the Father unlike anything the world had ever known, no one went back to reconsider the decision to crucify Him. As they overlooked Him in life, they forgot Him in death.

Isaiah 53:9 says, "His grave was assigned with wicked men, yet He was with a rich man in His death." What did Isaiah see? Yeshua was crucified in the center of criminals. We read in Matthew 27, "And when they had crucified Him, they divided up His garments among themselves by casting lots....At that time two robbers were crucified with Him, one on the right and one on the left" (vv. 35, 38). In death, Yeshua was dismissed as a common criminal, just as Isaiah predicted.

Stunningly, Isaiah not only saw Yeshua being linked to crooked men at His time of death, he also prophesied that Yeshua would be connected to a rich man in His passing. And as the prophet said, "He was with a rich man in His death" (Isa. 53:9). Jesus was buried in the tomb of a rich man, Joseph of Arimathea, fulfilling the prophecy.

> When it was evening, there came a rich man from Arimathea, named Joseph, who himself had also become a disciple of Jesus. This man went to Pilate and asked for the body of Jesus. Then Pilate ordered it to be given to him. And Joseph took the body and wrapped it in a clean linen cloth, and laid it in his own new tomb, which he had hewn out in the rock; and he rolled a large stone against the entrance of the tomb and went away.
> —MATTHEW 27:57–60

The agony that Yeshua experienced was surely fierce and abhorrent to God the Father. But because God is so relentlessly committed to our salvation and healing, Isaiah 53:10 says: "But the LORD was pleased to crush Him, putting Him to grief; if He would render Himself as a guilt offering, He will see His offspring, He will prolong His days, and the good pleasure of the LORD will prosper in His hand." The pain He experienced was beyond our comprehension. And it wasn't just the physical pain; it was that the innocent, spotless Son of Man allowed Himself to become defiled on our behalf. "He made Him who knew no sin to be sin on our behalf, so that we might become the righteousness of God in Him" (2 Cor. 5:21).

As Yeshua prepared Himself for the cross, He sweat drops of blood and sacrificed Himself for us, not under compulsion but willingly. Before being nailed to the cross, Yeshua said to His Father:

> Now My soul has become troubled; and what shall I say, "Father, save Me from this hour"? But for this purpose I came to this hour.
> —JOHN 12:27

> My Father, if it is possible, let this cup pass from Me; yet not as I will, but as You will.
> —MATTHEW 26:39

When we step back and consider the scale, scope, and preciseness of Isaiah's Messianic prophecies and exactly how Yeshua fulfilled each of them, it truly is astonishing.

We see again why Messianic prophecy does not merely engage the mind but builds faith, strengthening the fire of the love of God in our hearts. It is impossible for us as true disciples of Jesus to study the Hebrew prophecies of Messiah deeply and not be touched with the love of God!

## PURPOSE IN SUFFERING

While we see Yeshua in great anguish in Isaiah 53, verse 11 says, "Out of the anguish of his soul he shall see and be satisfied; by his knowledge shall the righteous one, my servant, make many to be accounted righteous, and he shall bear their iniquities" (ESV). Can you see why He was willing to suffer? In His suffering He has made "many righteous." His gain outweighed His loss.

Isaiah continues, "He poured out Himself to death, and was numbered with the transgressors...He Himself bore the sin of many, and interceded for the transgressors" (Isa. 53:12). Why would He do this? The very reason Yeshua came into the world was so that He could ransom us for the Father, set us free, and heal us.

As we think about the healing ministry of Yeshua and the effect it can have in our individual lives, consider the remarkable moment recorded in Luke's Gospel when Yeshua went into the synagogue, opened the Tanakh, and began to read aloud. When he came to the portion of the Haftorah (a short reading from the Prophets) and read from Isaiah 61, He ascribed it to Himself.

And He came to Nazareth, where He had been brought up; and as was His custom, He entered the synagogue on the Sabbath, and stood up to read. And the book of the prophet Isaiah was handed to Him. And He opened the book and found the place where it was written, "The Spirit of the Lord is upon Me, because He anointed Me to preach the gospel to the poor. He has sent Me to proclaim *release to the captives,* and recovery of *sight to the blind,* to *set free those who are oppressed,* to proclaim the favorable year of the Lord."

And He closed the book, gave it back to the attendant and sat down; and the eyes of all in the synagogue were fixed on Him. And He began to say to them, "Today this Scripture has been fulfilled in your hearing."

—LUKE 4:16–21, EMPHASIS ADDED

Yeshua does, in fact, heal the brokenhearted; He heals those who need to be made well. He delivers those who are oppressed. This is not just in some broad, generic terms, but in intimate, tailored, very personal ways, Yeshua brings healing to every individual soul who comes to Him.

We all need healing. It is not just an abstract "humanity" that needs healing—we all have a desperately personal need. The prophet Isaiah revealed that Messiah's ministry would heal the brokenness in the core of us. He would not come just to encourage us; He would set us free. He would not come to help us manage our broken pieces better; He would actually make us whole. In the same way that every person is affected by the same sin and brokenness, every person now through Yeshua has access to supernatural recovery, deliverance, and release!

It is possible for us to live with such security in Christ that we can continually love people without needing them to give us some kind of affirmation in return. When we are whole in ourselves because we know who we are to and in Jesus, we are free to truly love people. When we are able to love others without being held hostage to our own need to be liked, affirmed, or loved, we are, in the words of Jesus Himself, "Free indeed!" (John 8:36). The question for you and me is, Will we give ourselves wholly over to Him so He can make us truly free?

## A WORD TO THE REJECTED

If you are suffering the pain of any kind of rejection right now, I want you to know Yeshua is with you in your pain. He identifies with it—He understands it from the inside. There is no depth of human hurt that He cannot personally feel, sympathize with, and respond to.

As the winds of culture continue to shift in opposition to godliness, our identification with the rejected Messiah will grow as we stand with Him. It is never easy to face rejection and alienation; it is never easy to be misunderstood. But your obedience to God which results in suffering for righteousness may be the very thing that will take you deeper in your identification and relationship with the One who was "despised and rejected of men" (Isa. 53:3, KJV).

Beloved, we have been called not only to reign with

Christ but to suffer with Him as well. "Indeed, all who desire to live godly in Christ Jesus will be persecuted" (2 Tim. 3:12). "Blessed are those who have been persecuted for the sake of righteousness, for theirs is the kingdom of heaven. Blessed are you when people insult you and persecute you, and falsely say all kinds of evil against you because of Me" (Matt. 5:10–11). "But even if you should suffer for the sake of righteousness, you are blessed. And do not fear their intimidation, and do not be troubled" (1 Pet. 3:14).

The winds of change will continue to blow around us and become more hostile. But no matter how the world shifts around us, Yeshua, the One who endured such hostility by sinners against Himself, the rejected Messiah, will not change how He feels about you and me.

> For consider Him who has endured such hostility
> by sinners against Himself, so that you will not
> grow weary and lose heart.
> —HEBREWS 12:3

## COMING FACE TO FACE WITH THE SUFFERING SERVANT

In her book, *Treasures in Dark Places*, Leanna Cinquanta shares a powerful, haunting story of an encounter she had with God. I wanted to recount it here because the God she came face to face with is so clearly the God revealed to us in the song of the suffering servant in Isaiah 53.

As a young woman living with her parents in Minnesota, Leanna remembers a night in early spring, just after the sun had started to melt the snow. As a typical teenager, she loved to sleep late, but she woke up at five o'clock in the morning to premature rays of light filtering through the window, revealing shadows in the room. Though it was hours earlier than her normal wake-up time of 7:00 a.m., she was unable to go back to sleep. She stared indignantly at the ceiling, cursing under her breath.

Suddenly she heard an audible voice come out of the shadows: "There's someone in the guest bed."

"Who is in my room?" she wondered. She felt a sliver of terror at the thought that someone had broken into her room. Flipping over, she stared into the blackness of the shadows where the voice came from but saw no movement. That's when the words she heard began to register: "There's someone in the guest bed." Almost too frightened to look, her eyes darted over toward the bed only a foot removed from hers. What she saw made her cower back against the wall, stifling a scream: there was a hump under the blankets!

As she felt her heartbeat thunder, she was seized by terror: "Who is in my room?" she thought. "How did a strange person sneak into our house? Did we forget to lock the door? What might this person do to me?" The figure in the bed next to hers lay motionless, as if asleep. "What is it?" she wondered. "Human? Not human?" Feeling like she had to do something, she crept over the end of her bed, trying to stay as far away as she could from the unknown figure lying underneath the covers in the guest bed. Still there was no movement. She stood at the door of the room, ready to turn on the light, but she was too petrified. After standing there for a long moment, she slid back into bed and lay there paralyzed, watching and waiting.

The figure moved. He sat up on the side of the bed. That was when Leanna said her fear ended—she immediately recognized the man as Jesus. He was not the blue-eyed, blond-haired Jesus of art and 1950s cinema. She saw a visibly Jewish man of average height with olive skin. It was the Yeshua who suffered—the One we read of in Isaiah 53, His face bruised and blackened from repeated beatings. She could see blood caked in His hair and blood trickling from His wounds. His clothes were tattered and soaked with blood, His skin shredded.

Leanna describes a stunning moment of revelation, which I offer in her own words, as it is exquisitely told:

> With vehemence far eclipsing my former terror, now a revelation exploded through my being, igniting every sinew and synapse. Truth like an injection shot into my soul. Questions were obliterated and three grand and indisputable facts blazed neon-bright in my vision:
>
> GOD EXISTS.
>
> JESUS IS REAL.
>
> THE BIBLE IS THE WORD OF GOD.
>
> In that moment I knew that were I the only person in the world, He would have suffered this for me. He endured this for every person, no matter how good or bad. This knowledge

exceeded a mental persuasion. A surgical implantation had been sutured into my soul, a laser operation straight from the supernatural realm.

Usually if you do wrong and hurt someone, the person is angry with you. But in the bruised and scarred face of Jesus, there was no condemnation, no anger, but pure forgiveness and compassion.

I could endure only a brief look in his face. My mind swooned. Every muscle felt like water. *I am…in the presence of God. God in the form of a man…and He has suffered terribly to purchase my freedom!* The reality of it swirled in my mind and my body went limp. I fell on my face on my bed, weeping. The intensity of that moment is unexplainable and beyond words. My tears arose not so much from anguish as from awe and reverence, the single possible response for a mortal when found in the presence of the Holy One. But they were also tears of grief that such divine beauty had to be so marred for my pardon.

Then something happened that drove the experience still deeper.

He touched me.

He reached out His hand and laid it on my right shoulder. "My child, don't cry." His voice was gentle but strong.

My arms trembled as they lifted my torso from the bed. *It's too much for me*, I thought. *I cannot look into His eyes again.* But I knew I must. Like magnets they drew me. He had more to show me, more to impart. In His countenance, so tortured and yet so selfless, I beheld a love that no human can imagine.

But enthroned upon that love, a still higher revelation now pierced my soul. His sufferings' accomplishment exceeded personal pardon. A victorious light shone from His battered face, an aura of triumph and glory, the persona of One who has conquered all and now reigns supreme. The suffering He had endured constituted the price to rescue the world. I was witnessing the battle scars necessary to break the power of evil.

In a communication superseding words, buoyed up with a joyous lilt like the song of angels, I heard Him declare, *I've broken the power of darkness. The citizens can be set free forever.* Then His love was flowing into me, washing over me, waves of splendor engulfing my soul.

Placing my left hand on His while it rested on my shoulder, I felt the hole, where His wrist had been nailed to the cross. *This is not a dream!* My mind swooned again with the repeating fact. *This is real. I am not asleep. This is real. I am face-to-face with God!*[4]

When I read this in Leanna's book, I was pierced and struck. I believe this to be a genuine and real appearance of Yeshua, who is alive and still revealing Himself. While the visceral nature of Leanna's experience is extraordinary, the heart of it is not unique to her. Her encounter was with the living Yeshua that Isaiah 53 reveals to us. This same One who appeared to Leanna in tattered glory in her bedroom on a cold Minnesota morning in 1986 wants to reveal Himself to you and me now in a deeper and more remarkable way. As it was for Leanna, Yeshua visits us not to terrorize or harm us but to reveal the depth of His love. Do you intuitively feel Him calling to you now?

## SHARING IN HIS SUFFERING

Isaiah 53 is one of the clearest passages in the Bible through which we can recognize Messiah. It paints a sharp image of His nature and gives us a template or model for how to live our own lives. The apostle Paul told us that knowing Christ will entail not just the power of His resurrection but also "the fellowship of His sufferings" (Phil. 3:10). Notice how Paul personally embraced the concept of sharing in Christ's sufferings in his own life. "Now I rejoice in my sufferings for your sake, and in my flesh I do my share on behalf of His body, which is the church, in filling up what is lacking in Christ's afflictions" (Col. 1:24).

Paul gave up everything in life to do God's will and considered what he had given up as not worthy to be compared to what he had gained in its place. He had suffered the loss of all things but in the process gained Christ.

> But whatever things were gain to me, those things I have counted as loss for the sake of Christ. More than that, I count all things to be loss in view of the surpassing value of knowing Christ Jesus my Lord,

for whom I have suffered the loss of all things, and count them but rubbish so that I may gain Christ.

—Philippians 3:7–8

Following Jesus will cost us. Even as Yeshua gave up everything on the earth to do the will of His Father, so too in following Yeshua we must surrender everything. Jesus, in surrendering to the Father's will, went to the cross as Isaiah 53 describes. But the cross was not the end of the story. His resurrection and exaltation were. So too as you surrender to God and suffer rejection, persecution, or loss as a result, know that this is not the end of your story.

Remember the words of Yeshua:

> Blessed are those who have been persecuted for the sake of righteousness, for theirs is the kingdom of heaven. Blessed are you when people insult you and persecute you, and falsely say all kinds of evil against you because of Me. Rejoice and be glad, for your reward in heaven is great; for in the same way they persecuted the prophets who were before you.
>
> —Matthew 5:10–12

# CHAPTER 10

# A Light to the Gentiles

WE KNOW THE story of the God who brought the Israelites up out of Egypt. But Isaiah tells us that through the Messiah, this story of redemption would one day "cross over" to the other side of the known world, beyond the Hebrew people. In fulfillment of the prophetic promise God made to Abraham that through him "all the families of the earth [would] be blessed" (Gen. 12:3), God's message would cross over into the land of the Gentiles—to people who were not of Jewish origin or participants in God's covenant with the children of Israel.

> But there will be no more gloom for her who was in anguish; in earlier times He treated the land of Zebulun and the land of Naphtali with contempt, but later on He shall make it glorious, by the way of the sea, *on the other side of Jordan, Galilee of the Gentiles.* The people who walk in darkness will see a great light; those who live in a dark land, the light will shine on them.
>
> —ISAIAH 9:1–3, EMPHASIS ADDED

Let's look at the corresponding fulfillment of Isaiah 9:1–3 in the Brit Chadashah, the New Testament. Matthew writes, "And leaving Nazareth, He came and settled in Capernaum, which is by the sea, in the region of Zebulun and Naphtali" (Matt. 4:13). Then Matthew quotes Isaiah 9:1 verbatim, showing how this prophetic scene is fulfilled in Yeshua:

> This was to fulfill what was spoken through Isaiah the prophet: "The land of Zebulun and the land of Naphtali, by the way of the sea, beyond the Jordan, *Galilee of the Gentiles*—the people who were sitting in darkness saw a great Light, and those who were sitting in the land and shadow of death, upon them a Light dawned."
>
> —MATTHEW 4:14–16, EMPHASIS ADDED

Consider how remarkably specific this prophecy truly is. Isaiah tells us that the local ministry of Messiah would be in the small area of Galilee. From there it would spread and become glorious to all "nations." Messiah would not just be a light to the Gentiles in some broad way; after His ascension He would bring to them salvation and healing. Isaiah 42:1 foretold, "Behold, My Servant, whom I uphold; My chosen one in whom My soul delights. I have put My Spirit upon Him; He will bring forth justice to the nations [Gentiles]."

As a side note, consider this: Many of us rightly love Israel, and most who have been to the Holy Land especially love Israel's sacred city of Jerusalem. It is a dazzling, beautiful city, a place where so much of Israel's history and our future are bound up. Mount Moriah (where Abraham offered up Isaac) is there; King David's palace was there. But as magnificent as Jerusalem is, most of Yeshua's ministry was not in Jerusalem; it was in Galilee, just as Isaiah foretold. In fact, the predominant reason Yeshua went to Jerusalem was to be crucified there. Yeshua Himself said, "O Jerusalem, Jerusalem, the one who kills the prophets and stones those who are sent to her!" (Matt. 23:37, NKJV).

The concept of the Jewish Messiah being "a light to the Gentiles," although not fully understood by the Jews of Yeshua's day, is deeply rooted in the entire Word of God, as the following scriptures attest.

> Then in that day the nations will resort to the root of Jesse [Jesse is David's father, and Messiah Yeshua is "the descendant of David"], *who will stand as a signal for the peoples*; and His resting place will be glorious.
>
> —ISAIAH 11:10, EMPHASIS ADDED

> And there was a man in Jerusalem whose name was Simeon; and this man was righteous and devout, looking for the consolation of Israel; and the Holy Spirit was upon him. And it had been revealed to him by the Holy Spirit that he would not see death before he had seen the Lord's Christ. And he came in the Spirit into the temple; and when the parents brought in the child Jesus, to carry out for Him the custom of the Law, then he took Him into his arms, and blessed God, and

said, "Now Lord, You are releasing Your bond-servant to depart in peace, according to Your word; for my eyes have seen Your salvation, which You have prepared in the presence of all peoples, *a Light of revelation to the Gentiles, and the glory of Your people Israel."*

—LUKE 2:25–32, EMPHASIS ADDED

## SCANDALOUS GRACE

As mentioned, the Jews of Jesus' day did not understand the fullness of God's plan for non-Jews. In fact, for a devout Jew like Peter, who kept kosher and meticulously monitored his diet according to Jewish law, it would have been impossible to imagine that God could be calling him to places and people that were deemed ceremonially unclean according to purity codes. But the Book of Acts records how while waiting for lunch on the roof of his house one day, he fell into a trance and saw before him all kinds of animals that were not considered ritually clean for Jewish people to eat.

When he saw this scandalous buffet, he heard a voice say, "Get up, Peter, kill and eat!" Peter balked: "By no means, Lord, for I have never eaten anything unholy and unclean." Then the Spirit spoke to Peter and said, "What God has cleansed, no longer consider unholy" (Acts 10:13–15). While Peter was pondering what all this meant, suddenly there was a knock on his door—and it was a Gentile. This man said to Peter, "Come and minister to my master, who is a Gentile who believes in the God of Israel." (See Acts 10:22.) It was then that Peter realized the meaning of the vision—he was to no longer consider Gentiles unclean. Heeding this word, Peter went with the man to his master's house, and in doing this, the ministry of the gospel entered the Gentile world.

What Peter experienced here was a direct fulfillment of biblical prophecy. Speaking of the Messiah, Isaiah 60:3 says, *"Nations* will come to your light, and kings to the brightness of your rising" (emphasis added). Who are the nations Isaiah is describing here? This verse certainly isn't describing the nation of Israel, where God had already shone His light. These were nations that would be coming to see for the very first time the light of the Hebrew God, the light that was revealed to Abraham and Moses. These nations, of course, are the nations of the Gentiles. Scripturally speaking, there are only two classes of people: Jews and Gentiles. If you were not part of Israel, you were a Gentile—part of "the nations."

God's initiative to reach the Gentile nations through the Jewish Messiah is also demonstrated in the calling and ministry of the apostle Paul. In recounting his calling when on trial before the Jewish religious leadership, Paul said:

> "Brethren and fathers, hear my defense which I now offer to you."
> And when they heard that he was addressing them in the Hebrew dialect, they became even more quiet; and he said, "I am a Jew, born in Tarsus of Cilicia, but brought up in this city, educated under Gamaliel, strictly according to the

law of our fathers, being zealous for God just as you all are today. I persecuted this Way to the death, binding and putting both men and women into prisons, as also the high priest and all the Council of the elders can testify. From them I also received letters to the brethren, and started off for Damascus in order to bring even those who were there to Jerusalem as prisoners to be punished.

"But it happened that as I was on my way, approaching Damascus about noontime, a very bright light suddenly flashed from heaven all around me, and I fell to the ground and heard a voice saying to me, 'Saul, Saul, why are you persecuting Me?' And I answered, 'Who are You, Lord?' And He said to me, 'I am Jesus the Nazarene, whom you are persecuting.'

"…It happened when I returned to Jerusalem and was praying in the temple, that I fell into a trance….And He said to me, '*Go! For I will send you far away to the Gentiles.*'"
—ACTS 22:1–8, 17, 21, EMPHASIS ADDED

This is why Paul declared to the Gentiles while explaining the gospel and the person of Jesus, "'I have placed You as a light for the Gentiles, that You may bring salvation to the end of the earth.' When the Gentiles heard this, they began rejoicing and glorifying the word of the Lord; and as many as had been appointed to eternal life believed" (Acts 13:47–48).

In explaining God's heart, Paul wrote, "Or is God the God of Jews only? Is He not the God of Gentiles also?

Yes, of Gentiles also" (Rom. 3:29). This, of course, was the consummation of the promise that originated in God's covenant with Abraham: "In you all the families of the earth will be blessed" (Gen. 12:3).

Interestingly, it is precisely through the Jewish Messianic texts that we know the Messiah could not be the Messiah of the Jews only—He had to be the Messiah of all people. To say it another way, one of the primary ways the Lord gave us to recognize the true Messiah of Israel is that He would be revealed as the Messiah of everyone!

Yeshua's means of reaching us all was not accomplished by going high and targeting the elite and powerful but by condescending to the lowly (2 Cor. 8:9). This is one of Yeshua's most beautiful qualities. You and I also are being called to enlarge our hearts and in the name of Messiah love people who we formerly would not have felt inclined to love, for such is the heart of God. How big, how deep, and how wide is the ocean of God's love!

This helps bring us full circle to understand why God chose the Jewish people to begin with. He did not choose the Jewish people simply to be a special people who were unique unto themselves. He chose Jewish people to be the servants of the world, to be the priests of God to the earth—to bring the love of God to the entire world.

Even as the religious world of Yeshua's day did not have a paradigm big enough to wrap their heads around His ways and ministry, so too Yeshua comes to us now in ways that may defy our expectations. He still comes to redeem people whom we might dislike, to reach people we think are unreachable, to love people the world has deemed unworthy. He is still stretching the boundaries and the rules humans devise that keep people from encountering God.

# CHAPTER 11

# The Lord's Holy Days

IN THE TORAH we are given the foundation for the Lord's appointed holy days. Leviticus 23:4 says, "These are the appointed times of the LORD." People often think of these as Jewish holidays—and they are—but they do not belong to the Jewish people only. First and foremost, they are God's holy days. These holy days were first given to Israel, but their significance goes beyond the Jewish people. As Messiah was promised to Israel but was given through Israel to the whole world in order that "all the families of the earth will be blessed" (Gen. 12:3), so too these cherished days have significance for all God's people, Jew and Gentile alike.

These holy days have dual applications: they had immediate meaning for the people of Israel in their original, historical context, but also they are prophetic shadows of Messiah Jesus and in this regard have meaning and application for all God's people, including Gentiles. As is the pattern with Messianic prophecy, they had meaning before the coming of Yeshua, but the original significance is expanded and filled with new meaning in Him. In other words, the original purposes of the holy days are not minimized or any less weighted than they were before Yeshua came; rather, they are carried to their maximum, ultimate fulfillment in Him.

While many Christians today treat the Jewish holy days as if they are a mere historical footnote, their significance to Yeshua's entire ministry cannot be overstated. Every single one of the redemptive acts Yeshua accomplished in His death, burial, resurrection, and ascension and the sending forth of His Spirit were all strategically aimed to take place during the spring holy days as outlined in God's Word. Yeshua was crucified on the Feast of Passover, was buried during the Feast of Unleavened Bread, and rose during the Feast of Firstfruits. Then, after Yeshua's ascension, the Spirit of God came on Shavuot (the Hebrew word for Pentecost). Each of these feasts directly culminates in Messiah and prophetically tells the story of His life and mission.

## THE FEAST OF PASSOVER

The first of these feasts is Passover. We already considered the Feast of Passover briefly in previous chapters; this is the springtime holy day that commemorates the Israelites' deliverance from Egyptian bondage. In Leviticus 23:5 we read, "In the first month, on the fourteenth day of the month at twilight is the LORD's Passover." In its original context the Passover story is about how the Lord used the blood of a Passover lamb to deliver the children of Israel out of bondage in Egypt.

Each family would take the blood of an unblemished lamb and apply that blood on the doorpost of its home. When the angel of death, which was God's judgment, passed through the land of Egypt that fateful night, the judgment passed over every home that had been marked by the blood of the lamb.

The New Testament focus is that a new Passover Lamb has come. As Yeshua was about to begin His ministry, John the Baptist saw Him coming toward him and cried out, "Behold, the Lamb of God who takes away the sin of the world!" (John 1:29). This is book-ended in the Book of Revelation—the book of last things—where Yeshua is referred to as the *Lamb of God* thirty-one times. There are other references to Jesus in John's Apocalypse—such as "Bright and Morning Star" (Rev. 22:16, NKJV), "the Lion...from the tribe of Judah" (Rev. 5:5), and the descendant of David (Rev. 22:16)—but overwhelmingly, the emphasis on Yeshua is as the *Lamb*. He is the Lamb who was slain, the Lamb who is worthy, and the Lamb who sits upon the throne. Indeed, the people of God ultimately overcome the powers of sin and death through the blood of the Lamb. From the beginning to the end of the Brit Chadashah, Yeshua's role as the Lamb of God is central to understanding who He is and what He came to do.

Why do the writers of Scripture go to such great lengths to depict Yeshua as the Lamb when there are so many other ways He could be described? It is certainly not a way of saying that He was just warm and cuddly like a soft stuffed animal. The point is to demonstrate that He is the Passover Lamb that the Feast of Passover finds full expression in.

To highlight this point, John records for us in John 19 that Yeshua was crucified on Passover. There were times in the Gospels when the religious leaders wanted to seize Jesus, hoping to kill Him, but they could not because His time had not yet come. There is a distinct reason for this: it was not yet Passover.

When Yeshua celebrated that last Passover meal with His disciples, He lifted up the matzo and wine to tell them that His own body was about to be broken and His own blood shed, as He was going to give His life for their salvation. Paul wrote, "Christ our Passover... has been sacrificed" (1 Cor. 5:7). He was their Passover Lamb, and He is yours as well.

Consider that for ancient Israel, when the Passover lamb was sacrificed, it was not enough for the children of Israel simply to take the blood of a lamb and put it in a basin. They had to then take the blood that was in the basin and personally apply it, each one of them, over the doorposts and lintels of their homes. In the same way today, it is not enough for us just to theoretically or generally believe in the blood of Messiah Jesus. It is not enough for us just to believe He died for the sins of the world. We need to receive Him individually as our Savior and then take His blood by faith and apply it on our own hearts.

Similarly, during that first Passover in ancient Israel, every family had to slay its own lamb. This made it deeply personal. When it was time for the lamb to be slaughtered, the father of the home did not just take the lamb behind the house where no one could see what he was doing; he didn't try to shield and protect everybody from the lamb's suffering. Rather, the entire family had to take part in putting that lamb to death.

In the same way, it is our individual sins that put the Lamb of God to death. As it was for the children of Israel, when each person had to take part in putting that lamb to death, so too each one of us is responsible for crucifying the Lord Jesus, because it was for our sins that He was crucified. All of us are responsible for Yeshua's crucifixion. It was not just the Romans or just the Jews of the New Testament—it was your sin and mine that put Jesus to death.

Passover remains a remembrance of how God delivered the Israelites from the Egyptians through the blood of their ancient Passover lamb, but this first spring holy day is ultimately fulfilled in Yeshua, "the Lamb of God who takes away the sin of the world" (John 1:29). This is why Paul says Christ has become our Passover (1 Cor. 5:7).

## THE FEAST OF UNLEAVENED BREAD

Moving on to the second feast, Leviticus 23:6 reads, "Then on the fifteenth day of the same month there is the Feast of Unleavened Bread to the LORD; for seven days you shall eat unleavened bread." This feast marked a remembrance of when the children of Israel had to leave Israel in haste. During this feast, which begins the day after Passover, Jewish families remove all leaven from their homes and eat only unleavened bread, called matzo.

In preparing the children of Israel for their deliverance from Egypt, God instructed them, "When you hear My voice, *leave in haste* and do not wait for the bread to rise." (See Deuteronomy 16:3.) They were to instantly obey and move out. Thus, the Feast of Unleavened Bread speaks of instantaneous and full obedience. This is why Jesus was buried during the Feast of Unleavened Bread. Yeshua is the absolute fulfillment of this holy day, the One who perfectly and immediately obeys the Father.

During the last meal Yeshua shared with His disciples, He took the matzo, broke it, and gave it to them, saying, "This is My body which is given for you; do this in remembrance of Me" (Luke 22:19). The Feast of Unleavened Bread retains its original meaning for Israel and the Jewish people but took on its fullest and final meaning when Yeshua Himself, the bread of heaven, was broken and given unto us!

## The Feast of Firstfruits

I hope you can plainly see how each of these holy days corresponds to the person and ministry of Yeshua. The feasts of Passover and Unleavened Bread, respectively, take us into His death and burial. The next of the Lord's appointed days, the Feast of Firstfruits, carries us into His resurrection. We find this feast described in Leviticus 23:10–11:

> Speak to the sons of Israel and say to them, "When you enter the land which I am going to give to you and reap its harvest, then you shall bring in the sheaf of the first fruits of your harvest to the

priest. He shall wave the sheaf before the LORD for you to be accepted."

Each individual farmer—each worshipper—was to bring the first sheaf of the spring harvest to the priest, who would then lift it up and wave it before the Lord. The Lord would then deem the farmer's entire harvest acceptable and dedicated to Him.

Now consider again that this spring feast corresponds to the first fruit of the spring harvest. As I write now, it is still winter. I look outside my window to a gray and cloudy sky. There are no leaves on the trees. There are no splashes of green; there are no flowers; there is no fruit. The ground is all brown. It truly looks dead. But in a few months, when the spring comes, when the weather warms up and April showers water the earth, this dead-looking ground is suddenly going to be made alive. That which looks dead right now is going to come back to life. The grass will be green again; small, hopeful leaves will sprout from those dead-looking trees. Yellow, orange, and purple flowers will spring up from the ground, and fruit will grow on the trees anew. It will be like the earth has come back to life from the dead.

This all takes on new meaning when we see that Yeshua—who was crucified and died and was supernaturally raised from the dead—comes back to life on this holy day. Then He ascended to heaven as the firstfruits of those raised from the dead. (See 1 Corinthians 15:20, 23.) Yeshua said in Revelation 1:17–18, "I am the first and the last, and the living One; and I was dead, and behold, I am alive forevermore."

Notice further the timing of this feast. It took place on the day after the Sabbath, which is Sunday. On which day did Jesus rise from the dead? Sunday! Just as Yeshua became the unleavened bread that was broken for us, He became the firstfruit of the harvest brought back to life for us. As the ancient Israelites' sheaf was lifted up and waved before the Lord by the priest in order that the farmers' harvest would be accepted, so too Yeshua, the firstfruit of those raised from the dead, ascended and then presented Himself to the Father for us to be accepted. Just as in ancient Israel God accepted the whole harvest through the firstfruits offering, so it is today—we are accepted by Father God through the firstfruits offering of Messiah! Yeshua rose from the dead on the Feast of Firstfruits, both fulfilling it and bringing it to its capstone.

Jesus is "the firstborn of the dead" (Rev. 1:5) because He is the first in a long line of people (God's elect) who will be raised from the dead to experience the Father's love and presence in heaven forevermore!

## THE FESTIVAL OF SHAVUOT

The next feast is what we call in Hebrew Shavuot, which simply means "weeks." We call it weeks because it took place seven weeks and a day (fifty days) after the Feast of Firstfruits during Passover. In English we refer to this feast as Pentecost because Pentecost means fifty.

Leviticus 23:15–16 says, "You shall also count for your-selves from the day after the sabbath, from the day when you brought in the sheaf of the wave offering; there shall be seven complete sabbaths. You shall count fifty days to the day after the seventh sabbath." *Simplified, fifty days from the resurrection of Yeshua is when the day of Pentecost was being celebrated in Acts 2.*

Pentecost was originally an agricultural feast day, but over the years, traditional Judaism associated this day with the day the Lord gave the Law at Mount Sinai. During Shavuot we remember how God appeared in glory to the Israelites on Mount Sinai, giving them His law on tablets of stone more than thirty-three hundred years ago. Every year at this time, religious Jews renew their acceptance of God's gift, the Torah (the first five books of the Old Testament).

But a time would come when the Law and the lawgiver would draw nearer and become much closer. Jeremiah 31:33 says, "'But this is the covenant which I will make with the house of Israel after those days,' declares the LORD, 'I will put My law within them and on their heart I will write it; and I will be their God, and they shall be My people.'" Ezekiel also anticipated this time when he wrote that Yahweh would give His people a new heart and put His Spirit within them (Ezek. 36:26). The Law that was once written on stone would become etched in our hearts.

This was fulfilled in Acts 2, where we find 120 of the first believers in Yeshua gathered together in the Upper Room celebrating Shavuot. As they were there recalling once again how Yahweh appeared in fire on top of the mountain and gave Moses His commandments on tablets of stone, suddenly this same living God appeared to them afresh and anew—up close and personal!

As He did on Sinai, God appeared in fire there in the Upper Room. But it wasn't just one fire this time; rather, an individual tongue of fire appeared over each of the 120 who were there. This encounter inaugurated the time when the Lord would no longer speak to His people primarily by the writings on the tablets of stone. Instead, He was fulfilling the prophecies of Ezekiel and Jeremiah by communicating to His people from within them. This living tongue of fresh fire filled each of them. They had received the Ruach HaKodesh that the Lord Jesus had promised them.

> And behold, I am sending forth the promise of My Father upon you; but you are to stay in the city until you are clothed with power from on high.
> —LUKE 24:49

> Gathering them together, He commanded them not to leave Jerusalem, but to wait for what the Father had promised, "Which," He said, "you heard of from Me; for John baptized with water, but you will be baptized with the Holy Spirit not many days from now."
> —ACTS 1:4–5

> When the day of *Pentecost* had come, they were all together in one place. And suddenly there came from heaven a noise like a violent rushing

wind, and it filled the whole house where they were sitting. And there appeared to them tongues as of fire distributing themselves, and they rested on each one of them. And they were all filled with the Holy Spirit and began to speak with other tongues, as the Spirit was giving them utterance.... [Peter later explained to the crowd of onlookers], "Therefore having been exalted to the right hand of God, and having received from the Father the promise of the Holy Spirit, He has poured forth this which you both see and hear."

—ACTS 2:1–4, 33, EMPHASIS ADDED

To sum up, Shavuot, also known as the Feast of Weeks or Pentecost, reached its apex when Yeshua poured out His Spirit upon His church on this holy day.

## THE FEAST OF TRUMPETS

So let's review: Yeshua was crucified on Passover, was buried on the Feast of Unleavened Bread, rose from the dead on the Feast of Firstfruits, and sent the Holy Spirit on Shavuot (Pentecost). All these spring holy days that we have covered so far were fulfilled by Jesus at His first coming and happen within just a few months of one another. But interestingly, in the biblical calendar there is a long pause between the spring and fall holy days. This gap is prophetic and coincides with the relatively long period of time between Yeshua's first and second comings.

In the same way the spring feasts coincided with Yeshua's first coming, the fall feasts coincide with His second coming. Again, there is a pause in the biblical calendar between the last of the spring feasts (Shavuot/Pentecost) and the first of the fall feasts, the Feast of Trumpets, which symbolizes and reveals the relatively long time period (to us) between Yeshua's first and second appearances.

Leviticus 23:24 says, "In the seventh month on the first of the month you shall have a rest, a *reminder* by blowing of *trumpets*, a holy convocation" (emphasis added). Interestingly, there is actually very little told to us about this holy day called the Feast of Trumpets (Yom Teruah) except its timing (it is held on the first day of the seventh month, which in Hebrew is called Tishri) and the fact that it is marked by the blowing of trumpets.

But what is the blowing of the trumpets to remind Israel of? The first time the Israelites encountered their God, Yahweh, as a nation, the experience was announced with the blowing of a divine *trumpet*.

> The LORD also said to Moses, "Go to the people and consecrate them today and tomorrow, and let them wash their garments; and let them be ready for the third day, for on the third day the LORD will come down on Mount Sinai in the sight of all the people."...So it came about on the third day, when it was morning, that there were thunder and lightning flashes and a thick cloud upon the mountain *and a very loud trumpet* sound, so that all the people who were in the camp trembled. And Moses brought the people out of the camp to meet God, and they stood at the foot of the mountain.

> Now Mount Sinai was all in smoke because the
> LORD descended upon it in fire; and its smoke
> ascended like the smoke of a furnace, and the
> whole mountain quaked violently. *When the
> sound of the trumpet* grew louder and louder,
> Moses spoke and God answered him with thunder.
> The LORD came down on Mount Sinai, to the top
> of the mountain; and the LORD called Moses to
> the top of the mountain, and Moses went up.
> —EXODUS 19:10–11, 16–20, EMPHASIS ADDED

In this experience, the Lord revealed His glory to approximately three million Israelites who were gathered at the base of Mount Sinai. Consider again that in this encounter God announced Himself with the blowing of a *trumpet* that proceeded out of heaven.

As the trumpet that the Israelites heard from the heavens grew louder and louder, the Israelites, who were not ready to meet their God, just stood at the base of the mountain and trembled. But Moses, who was the humblest man on the earth, was ready. So as the trumpets sounded, instead of staying at the base of Mount Sinai, cowering in fear, Moses ascended the mountain and met his God.

Of course, this is a picture of the rapture. When Jesus returns with the blowing of a *trumpet* from heaven, those who are not prepared to meet Him will tremble in unspeakable fear. But those of us who are ready to meet our God will ascend and meet Messiah in the air. In 1 Thessalonians 4:16–17 Paul writes, "For the Lord Himself will descend from heaven with a shout, with the voice of the archangel and *with the trumpet of God*, and the dead in Christ will rise first. Then we who are alive and remain will be caught up together with them in the clouds to meet the Lord in the air, and so we shall always be with the Lord" (emphasis added). And he says, "In a moment, in the twinkling of an eye, at the last trumpet; for the trumpet will sound, and the dead will be raised imperishable, and we will be changed" (1 Cor. 15:52).

In both the past and future, the blowing of the shofar announces God's manifest presence. The next time God sounds His shofar/trumpet from heaven, it will signal the Messiah's return, at which time His glory will be fully manifested to the entire world!

As a side note, in modern-day Judaism this feast is also known as Rosh Hashanah, which means "Head of the Year," and celebrates the Jewish New Year. Traditional Jews believe God created the world on this day in 3761 BC.[1] A common custom is to say, "*L'shanah tovah*," which means, "May it be a good year." Another custom is to eat apples dipped in honey. The apples and honey represent God's provision and the sweetness we hope He will manifest to us in the coming year.

## YOM KIPPUR

The Feast of Trumpets is followed by the next fall holy day, Yom Kippur, the Day of Atonement. *Yom* means "day," and *kippur* means "covering," so this is literally "the day of covering." The fall days that begin with the

Feast of Trumpets and end with the Day of Atonement are called the Days of Awe. They are days of self-examination. During this time, religious Jews seek to make any needed corrections in their relationships with their Creator and with their fellow man. We read in Leviticus 23:27, "On exactly the tenth day of this seventh month [still the month of Tishri] is the day of atonement; it shall be a holy convocation for you, and you shall humble your souls and present an offering by fire to the LORD."

As we read earlier, on the Day of Atonement the high priest would go into the Holy of Holies, a sacred room that was initially in the back of the Tabernacle. When the Tabernacle became a permanent structure in Israel, it became the Temple. At the very back of the Tabernacle, and then later the Temple, was the room called the Holy of Holies, where the Ark of the Covenant, which housed the Ten Commandments, was kept. On Yom Kippur, the Day of Atonement, the high priest would take the blood of a bull and the blood of a goat into the Holy of Holies and pour it on top of the Ark of the Covenant, which in the Book of Hebrews is called the Mercy Seat (Heb. 9:5), as stated in chapter 3.

When the Lord saw the blood poured out upon the Mercy Seat, He overlooked the sins of His people for a year. The Day of Atonement is *all about the blood* that is shed for the forgiveness and covering of sin. The Lord can be in covenant only with humanity, whom He created in His own image, through a blood atonement, for "without shedding of blood there is no forgiveness" (Heb. 9:22).

> For the life of the flesh is in the blood, and I have given it to you on the altar to make atonement for your souls; for it is the blood by reason of the life that makes atonement.
>
> —LEVITICUS 17:11

> ...for this is My blood of the covenant, which is poured out for many for forgiveness of sins.
>
> —MATTHEW 26:28

Some theologians trace the blood covenant all the way back to the Book of Genesis, when Adam and Eve sinned and then were covered with animal skins, which required the animal to be put to death (shedding its blood).

In the old covenant the high priest had to take the blood of a bull and a goat into the Holy of Holies afresh every year. The reason the high priest of Israel had to do this every year is that the blood of the bull and goat were only symbols that could never permanently remove sin. Their blood was just a shadow or a type, so it had to be repeated. The blood of those animals was much like a credit card. The card itself doesn't have any real value, but the merchant accepts it because he knows the real payment is coming. So too the blood of bulls and goats presented on Yom Kippur did not have intrinsic value. It was a type or a shadow of the real payment that was coming—the blood of Yeshua, which took away our sin once and for all.

This is why we read in Matthew 27 that when Yeshua

was crucified, the veil in the Temple that separated mankind from the Holy of Holies was ripped in two.

> About the ninth hour Jesus cried out with a loud voice, saying, "Eli, Eli, lama sabachthani?" that is, "My God, My God, why have You forsaken Me?" And some of those who were standing there, when they heard it, began saying, "This man is calling for Elijah." Immediately one of them ran, and taking a sponge, he filled it with sour wine and put it on a reed, and gave Him a drink. But the rest of them said, "Let us see whether Elijah will come to save Him." And Jesus cried out again with a loud voice, and yielded up His spirit. And behold, *the veil of the temple was torn in two* from top to bottom; and the earth shook and the rocks were split.
>
> —MATTHEW 27:46–51, EMPHASIS ADDED

The blood of the sinless One was poured out, opening the way for us to be in relationship with God forever. This is why Hebrews 13:20 calls the blood of Yeshua "the blood of the eternal covenant."

In one way, the feast has been fulfilled insofar as Yeshua's blood has already been shed and we are able to be in fellowship with God now. But there is also a prophetic way that Yom Kippur too will find its ultimate fulfillment yet in the future. We will explore this more in depth in chapter 12, but this future fulfillment of the Day of Atonement takes place when the Jewish people turn to Messiah Yeshua.

Zechariah 12:10 says, "I will pour out on the house of David and on the inhabitants of Jerusalem, the Spirit of grace and of supplication, so that they will look on Me whom they have pierced; and they will mourn for Him, as one mourns for an only son, and they will weep bitterly over Him like the bitter weeping over a firstborn."

When Yeshua returns, He will lift the veil from their eyes! The Book of Revelation foretells this glorious event that Zechariah wrote about: "Behold, He is coming with the clouds, and every eye will see Him, *even those who pierced Him*; and all the tribes of the earth will mourn over Him. So it is to be. Amen" (Rev. 1:7, emphasis added).

Paul also foretells of this event in Romans 11, stating that at Messiah's return "all Israel will be saved; just as it is written, 'The Deliverer will come from Zion, He will remove ungodliness from Jacob. This is My covenant with them, when I take away their sins'" (vv. 26–27).

The Hebrew Scriptures and the New Testament alike anticipate a time in the future when a mass of Jewish people will receive Yeshua as their Messiah. As they do, the kingdom of God will be fully inaugurated in the earth and the fullness of the Day of Atonement will be gloriously manifest.

## THE FEAST OF SUKKOT

The last of the fall feasts is called Sukkot, the Feast of Tabernacles. This feast is a joyous time of giving thanks to God for His provision. We read about this feast in Leviticus 23:34–42:

> On the fifteenth of this seventh month is the Feast of
> Booths [Tabernacles] for seven days to the LORD....
> You shall thus celebrate it as a feast to the LORD....
> It shall be a perpetual statute throughout your gen-
> erations....You shall live in booths for seven days.

During this feast, at many Jewish homes and synagogues, a sukkah—meaning a tabernacle or booth—is
built out of lumber, grass, or any other natural sub-
stance and serves as a temporary structure. It is then
decorated with natural materials such as tree branches,
leaves, flowers, vegetables, and fruit.

Many people will eat their meals and sleep in the
sukkah for the entire seven days of the feast. While
in the sukkah, Jewish people remember how they had
nothing but God in their forty years of wandering in the
wilderness after coming out of Egypt. They lived in these
temporary structures and had no insurance policies. For
forty years God supplied their every need. He fed them
supernaturally with manna, gave them water out of a
rock, and caused their clothes not to wear out. They had
nothing but God—but He was enough! So now once a
year the children of Israel build these temporary shel-
ters, or booths, to remember the time in the wilderness
when God was all they had to cling to. This is another
beautiful foreshadowing of how we should live our lives
today—totally dependent on God.

Relating the Israelites' forty-year wilderness wandering—when they lived in the tabernacles, or booths—
to Messiah Jesus, Paul wrote this:

> For I do not want you to be unaware, brethren, that our fathers were all under the cloud and all passed through the sea; and all were baptized into Moses in the cloud and in the sea; and all ate the same spiritual food; and all drank the same spiritual drink, for they were drinking from a spiritual rock which followed them; *and the rock was Christ.*
> —1 CORINTHIANS 10:1–4, EMPHASIS ADDED

Likewise, Yeshua is our manna in the wilderness. He is the bread for our journey that is sustaining us now. He taught us to live in total dependence, teaching us to pray, "Give us this day our daily bread" (Matt. 6:11). Beloved, God will be enough for us today, even as He was for the Israelites during their forty years in the wilderness. Let's trust Him.

Sukkot, or the Feast of Tabernacles, also involves the tradition of the waving of the lulav. The lulav is made with the palm branch, along with the myrtle bough, willow branch, and etrog, or citron fruit: "Now on the first day you shall take for yourselves the foliage of beautiful trees, palm branches and boughs of leafy trees and willows of the brook, and you shall rejoice before the LORD your God for seven days" (Lev. 23:40). We hold the lulav up and wave it before the Lord. We wave it to the east, south, west, and north, and up and down, testifying that God is everywhere and that all good gifts we have received come from Him!

Most importantly, the Feast of Tabernacles reminds us how the Lord was with His people during their wilderness journey. His presence was seen 24/7, each and every day, for forty years as a pillar of fire by night and a glory cloud hovering over the Tabernacle by day. Similarly, God's presence is with you and me right now wherever we go—and will be to the very end of our lives. This is why Yeshua said, "I am with you always, even to the end of the age" (Matt. 28:20). My friend, if He is "with you always," He is with you right now!

## Yeshua in the Temple during the Feast of Tabernacles

In John 7, on the last day of the Feast of Tabernacles, Jesus cried out as He taught in the Temple among the people.

> Now on the last day, the great day of the feast [the Feast of Tabernacles], Jesus stood and cried out, saying, "If anyone is thirsty, let him come to Me and drink. He who believes in Me, as the Scripture said, 'From his innermost being will flow rivers of living water.'" But this He spoke of the Spirit, whom those who believed in Him were to receive; for the Spirit was not yet given, because Jesus was not yet glorified.
>
> Some of the people therefore, when they heard these words, were saying, "This certainly is the Prophet." Others were saying, "This is the Christ." Still others were saying, "Surely the Christ is not going to come from Galilee, is He? Has not the Scripture said that the Christ comes from the descendants of David, and from Bethlehem, the

village where David was?" So a division occurred in the crowd because of Him. Some of them wanted to seize Him, but no one laid hands on Him.

—JOHN 7:37–44

Notice in John 7:40 that there was a controversy as to whether Yeshua was "the Prophet." This term, "the Prophet," is taken from the Torah in Deuteronomy 18, where Moses said, "The LORD your God will raise up for you a prophet like me from among you, from your countrymen, you shall listen to him" (v. 15). Peter quoted that passage of Scripture in the second sermon he preached to the Jewish people.

The God of Abraham, Isaac and Jacob, the God of our fathers, has glorified His servant Jesus, the one whom you delivered and disowned in the presence of Pilate, when he had decided to release Him. But you disowned the Holy and Righteous One and asked for a murderer to be granted to you, but put to death the Prince of life, the one whom God raised from the dead, a fact to which we are witnesses. And on the basis of faith in His name, it is the name of Jesus which has strengthened this man whom you see and know; and the faith which comes through Him has given him this perfect health in the presence of you all.

And now, brethren, I know that you acted in ignorance, just as your rulers did also. But the things which God announced beforehand by the mouth of all the prophets, that His Christ would suffer, He has thus fulfilled. Therefore repent and return, so that your sins may be wiped away, in order that times of refreshing may come from the presence of the Lord; and that He may send Jesus, the Christ appointed for you, whom heaven must receive until the period of restoration of all things about which God spoke by the mouth of His holy prophets from ancient time. Moses said, "The Lord God will raise up for you a prophet like me from your brethren; to Him you shall give heed to everything He says to you. And it will be that every soul that does not heed that prophet shall be utterly destroyed from among the people."

—ACTS 3:13–23

The point is that in John 7, as Yeshua taught in the Temple during the Feast of Tabernacles, the debate among His hearers was whether He was "the Prophet" that Moses wrote of. Peter identified Him as "the One."

## Yeshua and the final fulfillment of the Feast of Tabernacles

The Feast of Tabernacles too will find its ultimate fulfillment when Yeshua reigns in the new heaven and the new earth, tabernacling with His people in the fullest sense, as the following passage attests.

Then I saw a new heaven and a new earth; for the first heaven and the first earth passed away, and there is no longer any sea. And I saw the holy city, new Jerusalem, coming down out of heaven from God, made ready as a bride adorned for her husband. And I heard a loud voice from the throne, saying, *"Behold, the tabernacle of God is among men, and He will dwell among them,* and they shall be His people, and God Himself will be among them, and He will wipe away every tear from their eyes; and there will no longer be any death; there will no longer be any mourning, or crying, or pain; the first things have passed away."

And He who sits on the throne said, "Behold, I am making all things new." And He said, "Write, for these words are faithful and true." Then He said to me, "It is done. I am the Alpha and the Omega, the beginning and the end. I will give to the one who thirsts from the spring of the water of life without cost. He who overcomes will inherit these things, and I will be his God and he will be My son."

—REVELATION 21:1–7, EMPHASIS ADDED

## GOD'S DAYS

I believe that in remembering and honoring these holy days, which the Lord calls His appointed days, we participate in a channel of blessing. In seeing how Yeshua has exclusively fulfilled the spring feast days in His first coming, our faith is kindled and quickened, causing us to anticipate and look for His return, when He will climactically fulfill the fall holy days. All of us, Jew and Gentile alike, who are in relationship with Yahweh through Jesus have been grafted into the commonwealth of Israel as well. Thus, these days are now for all God's people!

In cherishing these special days, we are being trained to consecrate all our time here on earth as holy.

Most importantly for this book, my purpose in reviewing the holy days of the Lord is to show you that these holy days are all Messianic prophecies that point to and find their final actualization and consummation in Yeshua. All these holy days—from Passover to Sukkot—are foreshadowings of Messiah.

# CHAPTER 12

# God's Plan for Jewish People

I N DEUTERONOMY 32, in what is referred to as the Song of Moses, there is a mysterious and often overlooked passage. Most people, when they read through their Bibles, will likely gloss right over it. The passage I am referring to is Deuteronomy 32:8–9 (emphasis added):

> When the Most High gave the nations their inheritance, when He separated the sons of man, *He set the boundaries of the peoples according to the number of the sons of Israel.* For the LORD's portion is His people; Jacob is the allotment of His inheritance.

This is creation language that comes from the Torah, the foundation of God's Word. When God created the world—when He created the sons of men, setting the boundaries of the nations—He did so with Israel as the nexus. Israel was the center and will always be at the core of God's redemptive plan.

This is why Yeshua will not return until Israel, which is the locus of the world, receives Him. When Yeshua came as Israel's promised Messiah, He told His own Jewish people, "You will not see Me again until you are saying, '*Baruch haba b'Shem Adonai*' [Blessed is He who comes in the name of the Lord]." (See Matthew 23:39.) In other words, Yeshua said He will not return until His Jewish kinsmen in the flesh receive Him. Yeshua said, in essence, "I am not coming back until My own people, the Hebrews, call upon Me to return." God's redemptive purposes are so intricately tied to the Jewish people that Messiah will not come for the second time until Israel cries out for Him.

We can see, then, why it is so disconcerting that many Gentile believers now believe and act as if Israel no longer has a place in God's heart or plan. It is easy to attend a church for many years and never hear anything taught about Israel. We often hear teaching about how the kingdom of God is here and now, life in the Spirit, how to be successful and happy, and all sorts of Charismatic gifts— yet Israel is too often left completely out of the picture. But from the writings of the Hebrew Bible to the writings of Paul in the New Testament, we see that God Himself has never left Israel out of the picture. God has never forgotten or simply moved on from His first-covenant people or the promises He made first to them.

God's unique promise to Israel need not threaten anyone else. Israel's special role doesn't mean that those who are not of direct Hebrew descent are *not* chosen; Israel's role does not mean others do not have a role. The issue is that when Gentile believers insist on being first, they cast Israel's God-given role out of their theology. Yet when Yeshua came, He came first to His own people. Salvation is "to the Jew first and also to the Greek" (Rom. 1:16). Jesus and Paul came first to the Jews, and from there the gospel spread to the rest of the world.

Consider Jesus' words as He walked upon the earth:

> But He answered and said, "I was sent only to the lost sheep of the house of Israel."
>
> —MATTHEW 15:24

> These twelve Jesus sent out after instructing them: "Do not go in the way of the Gentiles, and do not enter any city of the Samaritans; but rather go to the lost sheep of the house of Israel."
>
> —MATTHEW 10:5–6

> You shall be My witnesses both in Jerusalem, and in all Judea and Samaria, and even to the remotest part of the earth.
>
> —ACTS 1:8

## GOD'S COVENANT PROMISE STILL REMAINS

In Genesis 12:7 God says, "To your descendants I will give this land." This was a specific, actual geographical land that was promised to Abraham. After telling Abraham to look northward, southward, eastward, and westward, God further tells him, "Arise, walk about the land through its length and breadth; for I will give it to you" (Gen. 13:17). This particular promise to Israel is impossible to discount.

This is not just an initial promise that we are free to now ignore but a theme that runs through the entire Bible, both the Old and New Testaments.

Read with me this mind-blowing promise God makes to Israel from the Book of Ezekiel:

> Then He said to me, "Son of man, these bones are the whole house of Israel; behold, they say, 'Our bones are dried up and our hope has perished. We are completely cut off.' Therefore prophesy and say to them, 'Thus says the Lord GOD, "Behold, I will open your graves and cause you to come up out of your graves, My people; and I will bring you into the land of Israel. Then you will know that I am the LORD, when I have opened your graves and caused you to come up out of your graves, My people. I will put My Spirit within you and you will come to life, and I will place you on your own land. Then you will know that I, the LORD, have spoken and done it," declares the LORD.'"
>
> —EZEKIEL 37:11–14

To the prophet Jeremiah, the Lord said:

> "Therefore behold, days are coming," declares the LORD, "when it will no longer be said, 'As the LORD lives, who brought up the sons of Israel out of the land of Egypt,' but, 'As the LORD lives, who brought up the sons of Israel from the land of the north and from all the countries where He had banished them.' *For I will restore them to their own land which I gave to their fathers.*"
>
> —JEREMIAH 16:14–15, EMPHASIS ADDED

I don't want to deluge you with an avalanche of Scripture, but it is important that you see how overwhelming this emphasis is throughout the Hebrew Bible. When we see how often and how forcefully God declares that He will keep His word to Israel, it is not accurate or genuine to disregard Israel's place in God's plan and heart.

For many modern Christians, Israel's place as it relates to God's plan is muddled and unclear. This is due in part to a misunderstanding among Jews and Gentiles alike regarding the concept of Israel being God's chosen people. This has led to division and conflicts between Jews and Gentiles that go all the way back to the New Testament writings and that continue even to this day.

Of course, the separate calling God had for the people of Israel, through whom the Messiah would come, was never supposed to make them superior for their own sake, as previously stated. Paul fiercely insists that in Yeshua the dividing wall between Jew and Gentile has been broken down so that all have become one in Jesus (Eph. 2:14).

Keep in mind that Paul himself was a devout Jewish follower of Yeshua, deeply trained in the Torah and the history and practices of the Hebrew people. He understood his own identity as an apostle for Christ in thoroughly Jewish terms, and he never minimized this. But Paul also was passionate that early Christ followers should not continue the kind of radical separation between Jews and Gentiles that was then common in the culture. So in Galatians 3:28 Paul makes a truly revolutionary statement: "There is neither Jew nor Greek, there is neither slave nor free man, there is neither male nor female; for you are all one in Christ Jesus."

No one in the ancient world could have conceived of anything like this—a community in which all people would be on equal footing, regardless of their social class. Jews and Gentiles, those who were enslaved and those who were free, and certainly men and women were not at all equal. The idea is that Yeshua eliminates the divisions between classes, disrupting the world's system.

Yet critically, while Paul maintains that those who are in Christ are one, he does not by any means minimize their *distinctions*. There are obvious fundamental differences between men and women. Despite the fact that today our culture tries to minimize these differences as it pushes "gender fluidity," where it is now left up to individuals to self-define whether they are male or female, the biological differences between male and female are obvious in the human anatomy. In the beginning, God created them male and female (Gen. 1:27). Paul was not trying to say that in Christ there are no *distinctions* but that there is no *discrimination*!

Similarly, Paul was not trying to do away with the distinction between Jew and Gentile. He wrote in his letter to the Corinthians that Jews who come to faith in Messiah Jesus should continue to live and identify themselves as Jews, and Gentiles who come to faith in Jesus should continue to identify as Gentiles.

Only, as the Lord has assigned to each one, as God has called each, in this manner let him walk. And so I direct in all the churches. Was any man called when he was already circumcised? He is not to become uncircumcised. Has anyone been called in uncircumcision? He is not to be circumcised. Circumcision is nothing, and uncircumcision is nothing, but what matters is the keeping of the commandments of God. Each man must remain in that condition in which he was called.

—1 CORINTHIANS 7:17–20

Paul did not want people to bury their heads in the sand and pretend that they did not have any differences. He instead insisted that individuals would not be discriminated against in Christ, for the things that make them different and that determine people's status would have no bearing on their status in God. This is why Paul rebuked Peter when he began to treat Gentiles as an inferior class of people and separated himself from them (Gal. 2:11–14).

Unfortunately, when people confuse discrimination with distinction instead of grasping the equality Paul had in mind, they neutralize the role Israel plays, thus minimizing the unique destiny God has for the physical descendants of Abraham, Isaac, and Jacob. Some churches even teach that there is no longer anything unique about Israel or the Jewish people and that because the Israelites initially rejected Jesus, the promises the Lord made to them have been taken away from them and are now given instead to the Gentile churches. This is called replacement theology.

While it is a marvelous message that all of us come to God on equal footing and that Jew and Gentile are one in Christ, the fact is, Israel has a specific part to play in the future of God's Messianic redemptive plan. The Lord did not do away with the specific calling He has had for Israel, "for the gifts and the calling of God are irrevocable" (Rom. 11:29).

## FULFILLING GOD'S PLAN FROM THE BEGINNING

The truth is, when the gospel of Yeshua is preached to Jewish people, it is ultimately a blessing to Jews and Gentiles alike. This is part of Paul's argument in Romans 11. If Gentiles were blessed because the gospel came to them as a result of and after the Jewish people rejected Yeshua, how much more will they be blessed when Jewish people receive Him?

Paul says, "Now if their transgression is riches for the world and their failure is riches for the Gentiles, how much more will their fulfillment be!...*For if their rejection is the reconciliation of the world, what will their acceptance be but life from the dead?*" He continues: "But if some of the branches were broken off, and you, being a wild olive, were grafted in among them and became partaker with them of the rich root of the olive tree, do not be arrogant toward the branches; but if you are arrogant, remember that it is not you who supports the root, but the root supports you" (Rom. 11:12, 15, 17–18, emphasis added).

The salvation of Israel is mysterious. Speaking to the Gentiles, Paul said, "For I do not want you, brethren, to be *uninformed of this mystery* so that you will not be wise in your own estimation—that a partial hardening has happened to Israel until the fullness of the Gentiles has come in; and so all Israel will be saved; just as it is written [in Isaiah 59:20], 'The Deliverer will come from Zion'" (Rom. 11:25–26, emphasis added).

The mystery at work here is how a blindness remains over God's chosen Jewish people that continues to this day and will persist until "the fullness of the Gentiles has come." I believe this fullness of the Gentiles is not just that more Gentiles would come to faith, but that Gentiles would fulfill their calling by reaching back to Israel with the good news of Yeshua. Paul knew that by preaching to the Gentiles, he would be setting in motion the means by which Israel would ultimately be reached. He said, "But I am speaking to you who are Gentiles. Inasmuch then as I am an apostle of Gentiles, I magnify my ministry, if somehow I might move to jealousy my fellow countrymen and save some of them" (Rom. 11:13–14). In other words, Paul's vision was that the Gentiles he was reaching and who were coming to faith through his ministry would be used of the Lord to reach Jews. The Jews had rejected Paul's witness to them. This is why God sent Paul to Gentiles.

Paul said this:

> "It happened when I returned to Jerusalem and was
> praying in the temple, that I fell into a trance, and
> I saw Him saying to me, 'Make haste, and get out
> of Jerusalem quickly, because they will not accept
> your testimony about Me.'"...They listened to him
> up to this statement, and then they raised their
> voices and said, "Away with such a fellow from the
> earth, for he should not be allowed to live!"
> —ACTS 22:17–18, 22

Even though Paul could not personally bring Jews to faith, those whom he was reaching could.

Still today, most Jewish people who come to faith in Yeshua do so through the witness of a Gentile believer. When I as a Jew witness to Jewish people, they often feel they need to defend themselves against me. But when a Gentile believes in Jesus and starts sharing his or her faith honestly and humbly, a Jewish person will sometimes be more open and receptive. So if you are a Gentile, remember that you have a unique call upon your life to share the good news of Messiah with Jewish people.

## LET'S REMEMBER

Although I have shared that many in the church have discounted the distinctiveness of the Jews and the unique role they still play, others have gone to the opposite extreme and have become so romanticized by the notion that the Jews are God's first-covenant, chosen people that they don't witness to them. Some think, "Who am I as a Gentile to talk to the Jews about Jesus?

They are the chosen people. I am not going to force my views on them." This kind of inferiority thinking is completely unscriptural. Yeshua said to the Jewish people, "Unless you believe that I am He, you will die in your sins" (John 8:24).

Jewish people must receive Jesus to be saved just like everyone else. Acts 4:12 says, "There is salvation in no one else; for there is no other name under heaven that has been given among men by which we must be saved." Either Jesus is who He said He is, or He is not. Paul said in Romans 1:16, "For I am not ashamed of the gospel, for it is the power of God for salvation to everyone who believes, to the Jew first and also to the Greek." Don't be intimidated.

You must walk in God's call upon your life and be His witness. Some who love God are so struck by the reality that the Jews are God's first-covenant, chosen people and are so focused on being liked and accepted by them that they shrink back from doing what God has commanded. Jesus said, "But you will receive power when the Holy Spirit has come upon you; and *you shall be My witnesses* both in Jerusalem, and in all Judea and Samaria, and even to the remotest part of the earth" (Acts 1:8, emphasis added). He told His disciples, "As the Father has sent Me, *I also send you*" (John 20:21, emphasis added).

So again, remember Israel in your conversation with your friends. Remember God's covenant people in your church. When you have the opportunity to support the often deeply unpopular work of proclaiming Yeshua to

Jewish people, offer whatever assistance you can, whether financially or otherwise, as the Holy Spirit leads you.

Through our study of Messianic prophecy we have seen that we need to be public and unashamed in our witness of and for Yeshua. Ultimately, the more He is proclaimed among the Gentiles, the more the light that first shone from Israel will be shone back to it. We need to be steadfast in our love for Jewish people, as God has not forsaken or abandoned His promise to His first-covenant people.

Let us come into alignment with the Jewish Jesus because when we meet Him, we are going to meet the One who identified Himself as "the root and the descendant of David" (Rev. 22:16). We're going to meet One who in heaven is called "the Lion that is from the tribe of Judah" (Rev. 5:5). And we will meet Him in the heavenly city called New Jerusalem, whose gates are inscribed with the names of the twelve tribes of Israel (Rev. 21:12). Whether we come to Him as a Jew or as a Gentile, we will all meet Him together.

I have taken time to include the role of Israel and the Jewish people in our study of Messianic prophecy because when Jewish people come to grips with the fact that Yeshua is the Messiah, it will bring into fulfillment the reality of the Messianic age to come.

> "For behold, I create new heavens and a new earth; and the former things will not be remembered or come to mind. But be glad and rejoice forever in what I create; for behold, I create Jerusalem for rejoicing and her people for gladness. I will also

rejoice in Jerusalem and be glad in My people; and there will no longer be heard in her the voice of weeping and the sound of crying.

"No longer will there be in it an infant who lives but a few days, or an old man who does not live out his days; for the youth will die at the age of one hundred and the one who does not reach the age of one hundred will be thought accursed.

"They will build houses and inhabit them; they will also plant vineyards and eat their fruit. They will not build and another inhabit, they will not plant and another eat; for as the lifetime of a tree, so will be the days of My people, and My chosen ones will wear out the work of their hands. They will not labor in vain, or bear children for calamity; for they are the offspring of those blessed by the LORD, and their descendants with them.

"It will also come to pass that before they call, I will answer; and while they are still speaking, I will hear. The wolf and the lamb will graze together, and the lion will eat straw like the ox; and dust will be the serpent's food. They will do no evil or harm in all My holy mountain," says the LORD.

—ISAIAH 65:17–25

What an exciting future awaits God's people, Jew and Gentile alike!

# CHAPTER 13

# The Gentle Nature of God

WE READ IN the Hebrew Bible that Messiah would enter the holy city Jerusalem seated on a donkey. The scene painted in the Book of Zechariah feels like a kind of coronation, yet it is very unlike what most of us envision when we think of the crowning of a king.

> Rejoice greatly, O daughter of Zion! Shout in triumph, O daughter of Jerusalem! Behold, your king is coming to you; He is just and endowed with salvation, humble, and mounted on a donkey, even on a colt, the foal of a donkey.
> —ZECHARIAH 9:9

Zechariah prophesies that the King is coming, but the way He comes will be subversive. He will not come with the kind of grandeur, pomp, and circumstance that we associate with royalty. He will come riding on a lowly creature, not on a "high horse." Like the other prophecies we read in Isaiah, we see yet another way Messiah came in a form that was so counter to expectations, He was easy to miss.

Yet while the King would come in lowliness and humility, His reign will be vast. Zechariah 9 continues: "He will speak peace to the nations; and His dominion will be from sea to sea, and from the River to the ends of the earth" (v. 10). His rule will be "from sea to sea."

Matthew's Gospel shares with us this extraordinary scene:

> When they had approached Jerusalem and had come to Bethphage, at the Mount of Olives, then Jesus sent two disciples, saying to them, "Go into the village opposite you, and immediately you will find a donkey tied there and a colt with her; untie them and bring them to Me. If anyone says anything to you, you shall say, 'The Lord has need of them,' and immediately he will send them."
>
> This took place to fulfill what was spoken through the prophet: "Say to the daughter of Zion, 'Behold your King is coming to you, gentle, and mounted on a donkey, even on a colt, the foal of a beast of burden.'" ...The crowds going ahead of Him, and those who followed, were shouting, "Hosanna to the Son of David; blessed is He who comes in the name of the Lord; hosanna in the highest!"
>
> —MATTHEW 21:1–5, 9

What is Matthew referring to here when he says, "This took place to fulfill what was spoken through the prophet"? He is referring to Zechariah 9:9, connecting

Yeshua to the fulfillment of this prophecy in a way that is distinct and exclusive—so our faith will be unshakable.

## A REVELATION OF THE CHARACTER OF GOD

Beyond the way the Messianic fulfillment of this scene reveals Yeshua as Messiah, it also gives us crucial insight into the very nature of God. Keep in mind Yeshua's words to His disciples, "He who has seen Me has seen the Father" (John 14:9). Whatever we see Yeshua doing in the Gospels reflects who God is! Paul said Jesus is "the image of the invisible God" (Col. 1:15) and the One in whom "dwells all the fullness of the Godhead bodily" (Col. 2:9, NKJV). The writer of the Book of Hebrews wrote that Yeshua is "the exact representation of His nature" (Heb. 1:3).

Sometimes people speak as if the God of the Old Testament and the God of the New Testament are somehow different, as if they fundamentally contradict each other. For example, many Christians speak as if the God revealed in the Hebrew Scriptures only cared about laws, regulations, and ceremonial purity, but not about grace and mercy. Or conversely people think the God revealed in the New Testament did away with everything connected to the Torah and is only concerned about grace, love, and kindness and not about purity, justice, or holy living. This false dichotomy is completely foreign to the Scriptures.

Yeshua said in Matthew 5:17–19: "Do not think that I came to abolish the Law or the Prophets; I did not come to abolish but to fulfill. For truly I say to you, until heaven and earth pass away, not the smallest letter or stroke shall pass from the Law until all is accomplished. Whoever then annuls one of the least of these commandments, and teaches others to do the same, shall be called least in the kingdom of heaven; but whoever keeps and teaches them, he shall be called great in the kingdom of heaven."

The roles simply do not contradict each other. Yeshua does not negate the Hebrew Scriptures but deepens and fulfills them. What is remarkable about the relationship between the Old and New Testaments is not their discontinuity but their continuity. Yeshua is not a course-correction to the God we read of in the Hebrew Bible; He is the full revelation of Yahweh!

> No one has seen God at any time; the only begotten God who is in the bosom of the Father, *He has explained Him.*
> —JOHN 1:18, EMPHASIS ADDED

If Yeshua does, in fact, reveal the Father, then what does Yeshua's fulfillment of Zechariah 9:9 tell us about the nature of God? Think about it, when Mashiach entered Jerusalem, He came riding on a lowly donkey, a beast of burden. He came humbly. He didn't come in pompous or obnoxious arrogance, reveling in the adulation of the crowd. He didn't even come demonstrating His strength, though we all know that His power is uncontestable. He came in gentleness and tenderness.

This is the same reality foretold in Isaiah 42:3, that when Messiah comes, "A bruised reed He will not break and a dimly burning wick He will not extinguish." He would be sensitive and caring. He would not be unnecessarily harsh, rashly plowing over everybody. He would not exert Himself in a way that may damage the vulnerable ones.

This is an astonishing perspective of the very character of God. The all-powerful One who has been from everlasting, the One who has always been, the One who could do anything He wants is gentle, sensitive, and humble of heart. I love David's words to the Father: "Your gentleness makes me great" (Ps. 18:35). The scene in Zechariah 9 is an unveiling of who God has been all along. He is all-powerful yet gentle in His core. He has made Himself one with us.

Allow your soul to be touched by this reality: the eternal God of the universe comes in a way where He has made Himself low enough for us to touch Him. The God who should be beyond our reach makes Himself available and sensitive to us so that we can actually touch Him.

When we choose to follow Yeshua even when it hurts, it moves His heart. He is not aloof or distant but is vulnerable and makes Himself available to us, just as we make ourselves available to one another. It is hard to comprehend that He is moved by our love and touched by our feelings. And here is another mind- and heart-bender: we can actually add to His happiness when we choose to love Him. Even though God is complete and needs nothing, there is a mystery in that the Lord actually receives joy when you and I love Him. I know for many of us this may seem far-fetched and require a paradigm shift, but consider that the Bible teaches that "there is joy in the presence of the angels of God over one sinner who repents" (Luke 15:10).

Stunningly, we are even able to make Him weep. When Yeshua's dear friend Lazarus had died and the crowd that had gathered expected the most brilliant teacher who ever lived to say something profound, Jesus simply wept (John 11:35). His response was not to offer superficial words or pat anyone on the head to make them feel better, but He allowed tears to fall from His face. In Yeshua, the Lord has united Himself to us in our humanity. He feels us and responds to us.

We can actually touch the One who made us. We can touch the One who made Himself low. Yeshua entered Jerusalem, as recorded in Zechariah 9:9 and Matthew 21:1–5, the same way He enters our lives now—in gentleness and humility.

## WHAT WILL YOU DO WITH THIS HUMBLE KING?

The question is, What will we do with this humble King? Will we humble ourselves too? Will we disconnect from everything that causes His heart to break? The One who asks for our devotion doesn't come to us harshly or demanding. Instead, our God comes with an invitation: "Come to Me, all you who labor and are heavily burdened, and I will give you rest. Take My yoke upon you, and learn from Me. For I am meek and lowly in heart, and you will find rest for your souls. For My yoke is easy, and My burden is light" (Matt. 11:28–30, MEV).

I hope you really hear those words—our God is "*lowly* in heart." The King who rode into Jerusalem on a donkey can relate to you. He wants to take your burdens and carry them with you. When we see Yeshua the way He truly is, we cannot help but love Him!

Let's close this chapter by praying this simple prayer:

> *Jesus, I love You. Thank You that I don't have to be afraid of You. Thank You that You know me, feel me, and don't condemn me. Thank You for receiving me. Help me to share my whole life with You. Teach me how to let You carry my burdens. Help me to walk as You do, in gentleness and humility.*

# CHAPTER 14

# The Greatest Prophecy

EVERYTHING JESUS DID was anticipated in the Hebrew Scriptures. On the day of Pentecost when Peter preached about Yeshua's resurrection, he quoted from the last four verses of Psalm 16.

> For David says of Him, "I saw the Lord always in my presence; for He is at my right hand, so that I will not be shaken. Therefore my heart was glad and my tongue exulted; moreover my flesh also will live in hope; because You will not abandon my soul to Hades, nor allow Your Holy One to undergo decay. You have made known to me the ways of life; You will make me full of gladness with Your presence."
> Brethren, I may confidently say to you regarding the patriarch David that he both died and was buried, and his tomb is with us to this day. And so, because he was a prophet and knew that God had sworn to him with an oath to seat one of his descendants on his throne, he looked ahead and spoke of the resurrection of the Christ, that He was neither abandoned to Hades, nor did

His flesh suffer decay. This Jesus God raised up
again, to which we are all witnesses.

—ACTS 2:25–32

David anticipated the physical, bodily resurrection of
the Messiah. This is remarkable. God gave David the
spiritual eyes to see that Messiah, whom David called
his Lord (Ps. 110:1), would be raised from the dead. In
Yeshua's day, the topic of whether there would be a
bodily resurrection was hotly disputed. We see this tension between the Pharisees and Sadducees in Acts 23
when Paul stood before the council of Jewish religious
leaders in Jerusalem.

But perceiving that one group were Sadducees
and the other Pharisees, Paul began crying out in
the Council, "Brethren, I am a Pharisee, a son of
Pharisees; I am on trial for the hope and resurrection of the dead!" As he said this, there occurred a
dissension between the Pharisees and Sadducees,
and the assembly was divided. For the Sadducees
say that there is no resurrection, nor an angel, nor
a spirit, but the Pharisees acknowledge them all.

—ACTS 23:6–8

So you see, the Jewish people two thousand years ago
had not universally embraced the idea of resurrection,
but David had revelation. He knew and saw in the spirit
that even after death, Messiah would live on.

Not only do we find deep within the Hebrew Bible
prophecies about Yeshua's resurrection, we also find

mysteries that the prophets revealed about Messiah's second coming and the millennial age.

Consider that Zechariah, the prophet who foretold that Messiah would come into Jerusalem riding on a donkey, also tells us how Messiah will come with glory at the end of the age. Though the prophecies are not far apart within the text, they paint starkly different pictures. We might even call it a tale of two prophecies.

In Zechariah 9, as we have seen, Messiah comes in meekness and humility. But just a few chapters later, Zechariah reveals that Messiah's glory will one day be revealed to the whole world.

> In that day His feet will stand on the Mount of Olives, which is in front of Jerusalem on the east; and the Mount of Olives will be split in its middle from east to west by a very large valley, so that half of the mountain will move toward the north and the other half toward the south....In that day there will be no light; the luminaries will dwindle. For it will be a unique day which is known to the LORD, neither day nor night, but it will come about that at evening time there will be light. And in that day living waters will flow out of Jerusalem....And the LORD will be king over all the earth; in that day the LORD will be the only one, and His name the only one.
>
> —ZECHARIAH 14:4, 6–9

The Hebrew prophet Daniel also bore witness to this reality when he saw in a vision that at Messiah's return,

His glory will so encompass the world that all humanity will acknowledge Him, Jew and Gentile alike. Daniel's vision is one of the most unique in the entire Word of God, and Jesus refers to it in Matthew 24 when His disciples ask Him about the end of the age.

Here is what Daniel wrote:

> I kept looking in the night visions, and behold, with the clouds of heaven *one like a Son of Man* was coming, and He came up to the Ancient of Days and was presented before Him. And to Him was given dominion, glory and a kingdom, that all the peoples, nations and men of every language might serve Him. His dominion is an everlasting dominion which will not pass away; and His kingdom is one which will not be destroyed.
>
> —DANIEL 7:13–14, EMPHASIS ADDED

Daniel literally saw Yeshua's second coming, at which time the Father will turn everything over to Him. Everybody and everything will submit to the "Son of Man."

Yeshua's description of Himself as "the Son of Man" in Matthew 24 brings us back to the prophecies of Daniel and Zechariah: "And then the sign of *the Son of Man* will appear in the sky, and then all the tribes of the earth will mourn, and they will see *the Son of Man* coming on the clouds of the sky with power and great glory" (Matt. 24:30, emphasis added).

## PASSOVER AS THE BLUEPRINT
## FOR THE SECOND COMING

You may have already studied what we call eschatology, which is the study of the end times. While I don't claim to have the inside line on precisely when Yeshua will return, I believe the Hebrew Bible gives us the pattern and the blueprint for understanding how the end times will play out. Consider this in light of the ancient Passover. Remember, Jesus is referred to as the Lamb of God thirty-one times in the Book of Revelation.

Track with me: The Passover story, which is the gospel in its primitive form, gives us a template to help us understand end-time events. The blood of the lamb, which brought about the Israelites' deliverance, was a type and foreshadowing of Yeshua's blood. In the same way, Pharaoh in the ancient Passover story is a shadow of Satan. Even as Pharaoh was a cruel taskmaster, beating the children of Israel down and oppressing them in darkness, seeking to bring torment and hardship into their lives, so today is Satan, who is seeking to bring the whole world under bondage and crush God's children in the earth.

And even as Moses became the deliverer God used to raise the Israelites up out of Egypt and lead them toward the Promised Land, so too Messiah Jesus is the Deliverer who brings the church out from under the darkness of satanic oppression into the very presence of God.

Now consider that before that great day of deliverance (Passover) thirty-five hundred years ago, Moses and

Aaron called down ten plagues on Egypt. At God's command, they turned the Nile River to blood, caused flies and lice to cover the land, caused giant hailstones to fall—and on and on it goes. In the same way, during the end times the two witnesses we read about in Revelation 11 will call down plagues from heaven upon the earth—just as Moses and Aaron called down plagues upon ancient Egypt!

The same things that happened locally in Egypt thirty-five hundred years ago during the Passover Exodus experience will happen on the whole earth as the time of Yeshua's return draws nigh. The same plagues that fell locally on Egypt will fall globally on the nations. During the great tribulation, not just Egypt but the entire world will feel the power of God's judgments.

You may remember that when Pharaoh pursued the Israelites, he chased them to the edge of the Red Sea. The people of God could not go backward with the armies of Pharaoh closing in behind them, nor forward with the sea looming before them. So God *supernaturally* parted the sea so the Israelites could pass through safely to the other side. *The parting of the sea*, which was the means of Israel's supernatural redemption, is a symbol of *the rapture of the church*! As the sea was parted and the Israelites were supernaturally translated to the other side, so too the sky is going to part for us, beloved, and we will be translated out of this world into the presence of God Himself—the ultimate Promised Land.

If the Passover does, in fact, serve as a blueprint for the end times, then consider the prophetic timing of these events. The seas did not part for the Israelites when the plagues began to fall, but rather after the tenth and final plague (the plague of death). In the same way, I believe the church will be in the world for many of the plagues that will fall upon the world during the tribulation. I am convinced that the people of God will be ultimately protected, but we will still experience the effect of some of the plagues, even as the Israelites did while they were still in Egypt for the first ten plagues.

Now, I do not believe the church will be in the world for what the Book of Revelation calls the seven bowls of wrath, which will take place at the end of the tribulation period: "Then I heard a loud voice from the temple, saying to the seven angels, 'Go and pour out on the earth the seven bowls of the wrath of God'" (Rev. 16:1). These seven bowls of wrath are the equivalent of God drowning Egypt in the sea. Think about the fact that the Israelites were in Egypt for the first ten plagues, but they did not experience the "final judgment" that fell upon Egypt when Pharaoh and his army were drowned in the sea.

Once again, in the same way, the church will be in the world for the first part of the tribulation but exempt from the seven bowls of wrath described in Revelation 16. (For a full treatment of this subject, please see my book *The Book of Revelation Decoded: Your Guide to Understanding the End Times Through the Eyes of the Hebrew Prophets*.)

Now this is a challenge for many of us because it does not promise that God will simply take us out of the world as soon as things get hard here. Instead I am saying we *do* have to be prepared for hard times. But we don't have to be afraid of the hard times because God is going to be with us!

I believe that the more we have need of grace, the more help God is going to give us. The darker the world is, the greater God's light is going to shine upon His elect. Far from being a thing to fear, I believe these hard times are going to bring the church together in unity, and we will see a greater demonstration of God's glory and miracles than we have ever seen before!

Yeshua isn't going to come again until this tribulation comes.

> But immediately after the tribulation of those days the sun will be darkened, and the moon will not give its light, and the stars will fall from the sky, and the powers of the heavens will be shaken. And then the sign of the Son of Man will appear in the sky, and then all the tribes of the earth will mourn, and they will see the Son of Man coming on the clouds of the sky with power and great glory.
>
> —MATTHEW 24:29–30

The application is that we need to be serious about living for Jesus today. We have to be ready to go through difficulty. While I don't believe anybody fully understands how the end times are going to work out, I have learned to trust the pattern of the Scripture in general—and the pattern of the Passover in particular. If the Passover pattern proved to be faithful to illustrate how Yeshua would appear and what He would do at His first coming, why would it not be trustworthy to demonstrate how He will come the second time?

If I am wrong, you lose nothing. All I am suggesting is that you get serious about living for God today. Then, if I am right and you end up going through the tribulation, if you take this word seriously, you will be more prepared and not caught off guard. On the other hand, if you don't take this word seriously, you won't be ready to face hardship as a good soldier of Yeshua. The Scriptures declare: "Through many tribulations we must enter the kingdom of God" (Acts 14:22).

Consider Jesus' words about the end times:

> See to it that no one misleads you. For many will come in My name, saying, "I am the Christ," and will mislead many. You will be hearing of wars and rumors of wars. See that you are not frightened, for those things must take place, but that is not yet the end. For nation will rise against nation, and kingdom against kingdom, and in various places there will be famines and earthquakes. But all these things are merely the beginning of birth pangs.
>
> Then they will deliver you to tribulation, and will kill you, and you will be hated by all nations because of My name. At that time many will fall away and will betray one another and hate one another. Many false prophets will arise and will mislead many. Because lawlessness is increased, most people's love will grow cold. But the one who endures to the end, he will be saved.
>
> —MATTHEW 24:4–13

I believe all this to be true, not because I arbitrarily want it to be but because I believe this fits the pattern so clearly laid out in the broader biblical story.

## Yeshua *Will* Come Again

The *good* news is that after all these things take place, Messiah Jesus *is* coming back. For most of us, it is easier now than ever before to sense that His return is approaching as we see what is happening in the world—the hatred, the division, the chaos, the breakdown of values, and the spread of disinformation through social media. Our technology seemingly makes us all more connected to one another, yet we have never been as divided. Our headlines are litanies of wars, political strife, racial hostility, animosity between the sexes, and fights over gender identity.

People wonder why, with all the scientific advancements and the unprecedented access to information we have, everything seems to be spinning out of control and more chaotic.

Beloved, it is because Yeshua the Messiah is getting ready to return. Let's examine the revelation the Hebrew prophet Daniel gave us.

> Now at that time Michael, the great prince who stands guard over the sons of your people, will arise. And there will be a time of distress such as never occurred since there was a nation until that time; and at that time your people, everyone who is found written in the book, will be rescued.

Many of those who sleep in the dust of the ground will awake, these to everlasting life, but the others to disgrace and everlasting contempt. Those who have insight will shine brightly like the brightness of the expanse of heaven, and those who lead the many to righteousness, like the stars forever and ever.

But as for you, Daniel, conceal these words and seal up the book until the end of time; many will go back and forth, and knowledge will increase.... But as for you, go your way to the end; then you will enter into rest and rise again for your allotted portion at the end of the age.

—DANIEL 12:1–4, 13

I don't know if it will be next week, next year, ten years from now, or a hundred years from now. I don't know when it will be. What I do know is that as surely as the Hebrew prophets foretold Yeshua's first coming and the events surrounding it, they also described the descent into chaos the world would experience right before His return—the things we are experiencing in some measure right now. Yeshua's coming is nigh.

I am not saying this to produce paranoia or panic but so you will be grounded and ready. The world will inevitably spiral into even deeper darkness. It feels like there is less and less for us to hang on to because, the truth is, our institutions, religious foundations, and political orders are all crumbling. All our systems and structures, even the basic values and assumptions that have held humanity up, are eroding at warp speed.

As people are constantly bombarded with conflicting sources, conflicting "facts," conflicting versions of world history, conflicting definitions of what basic words mean, and even conflicting versions of reality itself, they are rightly wondering, "Who can I really trust?"

If there is anything you take away from this study of Messianic prophecy, I hope it is this: *the Word of God is trustworthy and reliable.* You can put your weight down on it. You can depend on it with your life. It will orient you; it will anchor you. It is our lifeline.

And it is not just the written Word of God that you can trust—you can trust the living Word, Yeshua Himself. Just as death was not the end of the story for Him, none of the pain and trauma we experience on earth right now will be the end of our story. And we don't have to be overwhelmed by the world unraveling all around us. We have a blessed hope (Titus 2:13).

The prophet Isaiah spoke about a time when instead of violence, terror, and hostility on the earth, the wolf and the lamb will lie down together, and even animals will no longer prey upon one another (Isa. 11:6–7). It will be a time when "the earth will be full of the knowledge of the LORD as the waters cover the sea" (Isa. 11:9). As the earth is covered now by oceans, it will one day be covered by the Spirit of God! Now that is something!

The Lord will not tolerate all the injustice, wickedness, and pain forever. He is going to stop it. The prayer that Yeshua taught us to pray will be answered: "Our Father who is in heaven, hallowed be Your name. Your kingdom come. Your will be done, on earth as it is in heaven" (Matt. 6:9–10).

Heaven and earth are going to collide. Let's believe Yeshua's last words in the Bible: "Yes, I am coming quickly" (Rev. 22:20).

CHAPTER 15

# Twenty-One Fundamental Messianic Prophecies

IN THIS FINAL chapter, I want to summarize twenty-one fundamental Messianic prophecies in the Hebrew Bible and show how each is fulfilled in the New Testament. I have organized the Messianic prophecies in chronological order, starting with Yeshua's origin in eternity, continuing with such topics as what the Hebrew Scriptures taught about the genealogical line He would come through and the place and nature of His ministry, and concluding with the ancient prophecy relating to His return.

This chapter is intended to be a quick-reference guide that will build your faith and equip you to share it with others. First Peter 3:15 instructs us to "always be prepared to give an answer to everyone who asks you to give the reason for the hope that you have" (NIV). So let's dig in.

## 1. MESSIAH IS ETERNAL

Micah 5:2 prophesies of the eternal nature of Messiah, saying: "But as for you, Bethlehem Ephrathah, too little to be among the clans of Judah, from you One will go forth for Me to be ruler in Israel. *His goings forth are from long ago, from the days of eternity*" (emphasis added). Isaiah 9:6 strikes a similar chord: "For a child will be born to us, a son will be given to us; and the government will rest on His shoulders; and His name will be called Wonderful Counselor, *Mighty God, Eternal Father*, Prince of Peace" (emphasis added).

We see these prophecies fulfilled in John 1, which tells us that the man Yeshua is in fact the preexistent, eternal One the prophets spoke of: "In the beginning was the Word, and the Word was with God, *and the Word was God*....And the Word became flesh, and dwelt among us" (vv. 1, 14, emphasis added). Nothing existed before Him. Continuing in the same Gospel, John 8:58 records Yeshua's words, "Truly, truly, I say to you, *before Abraham was born, I am*" (emphasis added).

## 2. Messiah Will Be Called Immanuel, "God With Us"

Isaiah 7:14 tells us, "Therefore the Lord Himself will give you a sign: Behold, a virgin will be with child and bear a son, and she will call His name *Immanuel*" (emphasis added). Far from being a distant, abstract deity, the God who would be revealed in Messiah would be God with us. In *The Message*, Eugene Peterson translated John 1:14 this way: "The Word became flesh and blood, and moved into the neighborhood." A bit corny, perhaps, but you get the point.

Matthew, using the words of the prophet Isaiah, declares that Yeshua has fulfilled this ancient prophecy: "'Behold, the virgin shall be with child and shall bear a Son, and they shall call His name *Immanuel*,' which translated means, 'God with us'" (Matt. 1:23, emphasis added).

## 3. Messiah Is the Son of God

We have seen that the unique mark of Judaism apart from its rivals in antiquity is that it is monotheistic; the Jewish people believe there is only one God instead of many gods or a pantheon of gods. But we also see how hidden within the framework of the Hebrew Bible, the one true God of Israel has a Son—thus the mystery of the Hebrew prophecy of Psalm 2:

> "I will surely tell of the decree of the LORD: He said to Me, '*You are My Son*, today I have begotten you.'"...Worship the LORD with reverence and rejoice with trembling. Do homage to the Son, that He not become angry, and you perish in the way, for His wrath may soon be kindled. How blessed are all who take refuge in Him!"
> —PSALM 2:7, 11–12, EMPHASIS ADDED

These words of David find their direct fulfillment in Matthew 17:5 at the baptism of Yeshua, when He is revealed as the Son of God: "While he was still speaking, a bright cloud overshadowed them, and behold, a voice out of the cloud said, 'This is My beloved Son, with whom I am well-pleased; listen to Him!'" There is only one God, but this one true God has a Son in His bosom

(John 1:18) who is part of His existence and nature. In Luke 22:70 we read, "And they all said, 'Are You the Son of God, then?' And He said to them, 'Yes, I am.'"

## 4. MESSIAH WILL BE THE OFFSPRING OF A WOMAN

We have seen that the patriarchal ancient world was not always honoring to women. But Hebrew prophecy was distinct and clear that Messiah would be the offspring of a woman. The Lord said to Satan the serpent after he deceived Eve: "And I will put enmity between you and the woman, and between your seed and *her seed*; he shall bruise you on the head, and you shall bruise him on the heel" (Gen. 3:15, emphasis added). Notice here that it is the woman's seed that crushes the serpent.

We see this prophecy fulfilled in Yeshua being born of the Jewish woman Mary, which is recounted at length in the three synoptic Gospels of Matthew, Mark, and Luke. John's Gospel is a complementary rendering of the incarnation of Yeshua, emphasizing that the One born of a woman is also the eternal Word, who would overthrow the ruler of this world, Satan (John 12:31; 19:25–27).

## 5. MESSIAH WILL BE THE SEED OF ABRAHAM

Hebrew prophecy anticipated that Messiah would be the seed of Abraham, as we see in Genesis 22:18: "In your seed all the nations of the earth shall be blessed, because you have obeyed My voice." The Messiah could not come from just anywhere or anyone, but would have to be in the direct bloodline, the immediate ancestry, of the patriarch Abraham. Thus the very first verse of the New Testament—Matthew 1:1—drives home that Yeshua is Abraham's seed, fulfilling the prophecy, "the record of the genealogy of Jesus the Messiah, the son of David, *the son of Abraham.*" The apostle Paul likewise wrote in Galatians 3:16, "Now the promises were spoken to Abraham and to *his seed.* He does not say, 'And to seeds,' as referring to many, but rather to one, 'and to your seed,' that is, Christ" (emphasis added).

## 6. Messiah's Genealogy Will Proceed Through Isaac and Jacob

Most people know the three Hebrew patriarchs are Abraham, Isaac, and Jacob. The Torah is clear that the Messiah's lineage would continue down Abraham's line through Isaac and Jacob. In Genesis 17:19 we read, "But God said, '...your wife will bear you a son, and you shall call his name *Isaac*; and I will establish My covenant with him for an everlasting covenant for his descendants after him'" (emphasis added). And Genesis 21:12 says, "*Through Isaac* your descendants shall be named" (emphasis added). Then in Numbers 24:17 we read this mysterious Messianic prophecy: "I see him, but not now; I behold him, but not near; a star shall *come forth from Jacob*" (emphasis added).

Matthew is very intentional in his Gospel to make it clear that Yeshua has descended through the line of

Abraham, Isaac, and Jacob in fulfillment of the Hebrew Scriptures: "Abraham was the father of Isaac, Isaac the father of Jacob, and Jacob the father of Judah and his brothers" (Matt. 1:2). This prophetic thread and its fulfillment is also picked up in Luke 3:34, which tells us that Yeshua is "the son of Jacob, the son of Isaac, the son of Abraham, the son of Terah." Interestingly here, Luke goes on in his genealogical account and traces Yeshua's lineage all the way back to Adam (Luke 3:38).

## 7. MESSIAH WILL COME FORTH FROM THE TRIBE OF JUDAH

The Torah further clarifies that Messiah would come through the tribe that would grow out of Jacob's son Judah. Genesis 49:10 says, "*The scepter shall not depart from Judah*, nor the ruler's staff from between his feet, until *Shiloh* [Messiah] comes, and to him shall be the obedience of the peoples" (emphasis added). In John's apocalyptic finale, the Book of Revelation, Yeshua is specifically identified as the One Genesis 49:10 foresaw: "And one of the elders said to me, 'Stop weeping; behold, *the Lion that is from the tribe of Judah*, the Root of David, has overcome so as to open the book and its seven seals'" (Rev. 5:5, emphasis added).

## 8. MESSIAH WILL COME FROM THE LINE OF DAVID

Let's take a step back for a quick review. The Hebrew Scriptures prophesied that Messiah would come from

Abraham's seed or lineage. Abraham's son was Isaac, and Isaac fathered Jacob. Jacob then had twelve sons, and his descendants became the heads of the twelve tribes of Israel. One of his sons was Judah, and it was through Judah's line that Messiah would come. This was all prophesied in advance and is still affirmed by religious Jews today. But the Messianic prophecy is even more specific. The Hebrew prophets foretold that within the tribe of Judah, Messiah would specifically come through King David's family.

In Jeremiah 33:14–15 we read, "'Behold, days are coming,' declares the LORD, 'when I will fulfill the good word which I have spoken concerning the house of Israel and the house of Judah. In those days and at that time I will cause a righteous *Branch of David* to spring forth; and He shall execute justice and righteousness on the earth'" (emphasis added). Ezekiel 34:23–24 tells us, "Then I will set over them one shepherd, *My servant David*, and he will feed them; he will feed them himself and be their shepherd. And I, the LORD, will be their God, and *My servant David* will be prince among them; I the LORD have spoken" (emphasis added).

The New Testament repeatedly makes the point that Yeshua is from the Davidic line because it is such a critical detail in helping us to identify and recognize the true Messiah. (Interestingly, Yeshua's Davidic bloodline is traced through His mother in Luke 3, which I discussed in chapter 6.)

David said in Psalm 110:1, "The LORD says to my Lord: 'Sit at My right hand until I make Your enemies a footstool for Your feet.'" In the New Testament, Yeshua refers to David's psalm while being interrogated by a hostile crowd of Pharisees:

> Now while the Pharisees were gathered together, Jesus asked them a question: "What do you think about the Christ, whose son is He?" They said to Him, "The son of David." He said to them, "Then how does David in the Spirit call Him 'Lord,' saying, 'The Lord said to my Lord, "Sit at My right hand, until I put Your enemies beneath Your feet"'? If David then calls Him 'Lord,' how is He his son?" No one was able to answer Him a word, nor did anyone dare from that day on to ask Him another question.
>
> —Matthew 22:41–46

Note how directly Yeshua identifies Himself as having fulfilled the Messianic, Davidic expectation:

> "I, Jesus, have sent My angel to testify to you these things for the churches. *I am the root and the descendant of David*, the bright morning star." The Spirit and the bride say, "Come." And let the one who hears say, "Come." And let the one who is thirsty come; let the one who wishes take the water of life without cost. I testify to everyone who hears the words of the prophecy of this book: if anyone adds to them, God will add to him the plagues which are written in this book; and if anyone takes away from the words of the book of this prophecy, God will take away his part from

the tree of life and from the holy city, which are written in this book. He who testifies to these things says, "Yes, I am coming quickly." Amen. Come, Lord Jesus.

—REVELATION 22:16–20, EMPHASIS ADDED

## 9. MESSIAH'S BIRTH WILL BE SUPERNATURAL

The supernatural birth of Messiah was shadowed in the Hebrew Scriptures by the supernatural birth of Isaac, whom Sarah gave birth to when she was ninety years old. The Lord said to Abraham:

> "I will surely return to you at this time next year; and behold, Sarah your wife will have a son." And Sarah was listening at the tent door, which was behind him. Now Abraham and Sarah were old, advanced in age; Sarah was past childbearing. Sarah laughed to herself, saying, "After I have become old, shall I have pleasure, my lord being old also?" *And the LORD said to Abraham, "Why did Sarah laugh, saying, 'Shall I indeed bear a child, when I am so old?' Is anything too difficult for the LORD?* At the appointed time I will return to you, at this time next year, and Sarah will have a son."

—GENESIS 18:10–14, EMPHASIS ADDED

The Old Testament Scriptures taught that the Messiah also would enter the earth through a supernatural birth. Isaiah 7:14 says, "Therefore the Lord Himself will give you a sign: Behold, a virgin will be with child and bear a son, and she will call His name Immanuel."

This was fulfilled when Yeshua was conceived by the Holy Spirit and born of the Virgin Mary:

> Now the birth of Jesus Christ was as follows: when His mother Mary had been betrothed to Joseph, before they came together she was found to be with child by the Holy Spirit. And Joseph her husband, being a righteous man and not wanting to disgrace her, planned to send her away secretly. But when he had considered this, behold, an angel of the Lord appeared to him in a dream, saying, "Joseph, son of David, do not be afraid to take Mary as your wife; for the Child who has been conceived in her is of the Holy Spirit. She will bear a Son; and you shall call His name Jesus, for He will save His people from their sins." Now all this took place to fulfill what was spoken by the Lord through the prophet: "Behold, the virgin shall be with child and shall bear a Son, and they shall call His name Immanuel," which translated means, "God with us."
>
> —MATTHEW 1:18–23

## 10. MESSIAH WILL BE BORN IN BETHLEHEM

Hebrew prophecy specifically tells us where Messiah would be born—in Bethlehem. Micah 5:2 records, "But as for you, *Bethlehem* Ephrathah, too little to be among the clans of Judah, from you One will go forth for Me to be ruler in Israel. His goings forth are from long ago, from the days of eternity" (emphasis added).

We see Micah's words come to pass in Matthew 2:1–6 (emphasis added):

> Now after Jesus was born in Bethlehem of Judea in the days of Herod the king, magi from the east arrived in Jerusalem, saying, "Where is He who has been born King of the Jews? For we saw His star in the east and have come to worship Him." When Herod the king heard this, he was troubled, and all Jerusalem with him. Gathering together all the chief priests and scribes of the people, he inquired of them where the Messiah was to be born. They said to him, "In Bethlehem of Judea; for this is what has been written by the prophet: 'And you, Bethlehem, land of Judah, are by no means least among the leaders of Judah; for out of you shall come forth a Ruler who will shepherd My people Israel.'"

Messiah Yeshua was born in the precise obscure place that was foretold.

## 11. Messiah Will Be Preceded by a Messenger

Hebrew Scripture foretold that Messiah would be preceded by a messenger. Malachi 3:1 says, "'Behold, I am going to send *My messenger*, and he will clear the way before Me. And the Lord, whom you seek, will suddenly come to His temple; and the *messenger* of the covenant, in whom you delight, behold, He is coming,' says the LORD of hosts" (emphasis added). Not only did the Lord reveal through Malachi that He would send His messenger to prepare the way for Messiah; He furthermore revealed who this messenger would be—Elijah. "Behold, I am going to send you Elijah the prophet before the coming of the great and terrible day of the LORD" (Mal. 4:5).

In the New Testament we see this fulfilled through the wild man who ate locusts and wore camel's hair, John the Baptist, whom Yeshua declared was the Elijah that Malachi wrote of.

Quoting Malachi 3:1, John the Baptist said about himself, "I am a voice of one crying in the wilderness, 'Make straight the way of the Lord'" (John 1:23). Confirming John's words, Yeshua directly said to the crowds, "If you are willing to accept it, John himself is Elijah who was to come" (Matt. 11:14).

Jesus shed further light on this in Matthew 17:10–13 when the disciples questioned Him about the role of Elijah in relationship to the Messiah:

> And His disciples asked Him, "Why then do the scribes say that Elijah must come first?" And He answered and said, "Elijah is coming and will restore all things; but I say to you that Elijah already came, and they did not recognize him, but did to him whatever they wished. So also the Son of Man is going to suffer at their hands." Then the disciples understood that He had spoken to them about John the Baptist.

The disciples then understood the prophecies of old through the mouth of their rabbi. May you and I also be enlightened to see how Yeshua fulfilled this and other Messianic prophecies.

## 12. MESSIAH WILL PREACH GOOD NEWS

Isaiah 61:1 clarifies the mission of the Messiah: "The Spirit of the Lord GOD is upon me, because *the* LORD *has anointed me to bring good news* to the afflicted; He has sent me to bind up the brokenhearted, to proclaim liberty to captives and freedom to prisoners" (emphasis added). This has been fulfilled in Yeshua's ministry by the countless examples of oppressed, afflicted, brokenhearted, and beaten-down people who have found healing, freedom, wholeness, and hope in Him. This was the case two thousand years ago when Yeshua walked the earth, and it is still happening today.

Luke 4:14–21 records how Yeshua stood up in the synagogue and read Isaiah 61:1. Then, looking directly into His hearers' eyes, He said in effect, "This prophecy is fulfilled by Me."

> And Jesus returned to Galilee in the power of the Spirit, and news about Him spread through all the surrounding district. And He began teaching in their synagogues and was praised by all. And He came to Nazareth, where He had been brought up; and as was His custom, He entered the synagogue on the Sabbath, and stood up to read. And the book of the prophet Isaiah was handed to Him.
>
> And He opened the book and found the place where it was written, *"The Spirit of the Lord is*

*upon Me, because He anointed Me to preach the*
*gospel* [good news] *to the poor. He has sent Me*
to proclaim release to the captives, and recovery
of sight to the blind, to set free those who are
oppressed, to proclaim the favorable year of the
Lord." And He closed the book, gave it back to the
attendant and sat down; and the eyes of all in the
synagogue were fixed on Him. And He began to
say to them, "Today this Scripture has been fulfilled in your hearing."
—LUKE 4:14–21, EMPHASIS ADDED

Again, not only has Yeshua fulfilled this anticipated
hope historically, but He continues to fulfill it over and
over again today!

## 13. MESSIAH'S MINISTRY WILL BE IN GALILEE

Beyond revealing the nature of Yeshua's message (good
news), the prophets furthermore pinpointed where His
ministry would initially take place. Isaiah 9:1 foretold
that Messiah's ministry would take place in Galilee: "But
there will be no more gloom for her who was in anguish;
in earlier times He treated the land of Zebulun and the
land of Naphtali with contempt, but later on He shall
make it glorious, by the way of the sea, on the other side
of Jordan, *Galilee* of the Gentiles" (emphasis added).

Matthew 4:12–16 highlights how Yeshua fulfilled
Isaiah's words: "Now when Jesus heard that John had
been taken into custody, He withdrew into Galilee; and

leaving Nazareth, He came and settled in Capernaum, which is by the sea, in the region of Zebulun and Naphtali. This was to fulfill what was spoken through Isaiah the prophet: 'The land of Zebulun and the land of Naphtali, by the way of the sea, beyond the Jordan, *Galilee* of the Gentiles—the people who were sitting in darkness saw a great Light, and those who were sitting in the land and shadow of death, upon them a Light dawned'" (emphasis added).

## 14. MESSIAH WILL BE A LIGHT AND A MINISTER TO THE GENTILES

Yeshua's ministry and message would eventually spread beyond the Jews to include the Gentiles. Isaiah 60:3 says, "*Nations will come to your light*, and kings to the brightness of your rising" (emphasis added). Luke records how Yeshua's parents took Him to the Temple as an infant and a man named Simeon prophesied over the baby Jesus: "*A Light of revelation to the Gentiles*, and the glory of Your people Israel" (Luke 2:32, emphasis added).

We see this prophecy continuing in its fulfillment in the ministry of the apostle Paul. Through Paul, the gospel spread like fire through the Gentile world.

Messianic prophecy further clarifies that Messiah's ministry would also bring healing and deliverance to those who were once considered unclean. (See Acts 10.) We read in Isaiah 11:10: "Then in that day *the nations* will resort to the root of Jesse, who will stand as a signal for the peoples; and His resting place will be glorious" (emphasis added). In the New Testament we read Paul's brilliant questions: "Is God the God of Jews only? Is He not the God of Gentiles also?" (Rom. 3:29).

## 15. MESSIAH WILL ENTER JERUSALEM TRIUMPHANTLY ON A DONKEY

The specificity of Messianic prophecy is sometimes astonishing. For example, the prophet Zechariah foretold that Messiah would enter Jerusalem riding on a donkey: "Rejoice greatly, O daughter of Zion! Shout in triumph, O daughter of Jerusalem! Behold, your king is coming to you; He is just and endowed with salvation, humble, and mounted on a donkey, even on a colt, the foal of a *donkey*" (Zech. 9:9, emphasis added).

Incredibly, this very event happened and was recorded in Matthew 21:1–9. It is often referred to as Jesus' triumphal entry and is celebrated as the feast day Palm Sunday in some Christian cultures.

> When they had approached Jerusalem and had come to Bethphage, at the Mount of Olives, then Jesus sent two disciples, saying to them, "Go into the village opposite you, and immediately you will find a donkey tied there and a colt with her; untie them and bring them to Me. If anyone says anything to you, you shall say, 'The Lord has need of them,' and immediately he will send them." This took place to fulfill what was spoken through the prophet: "Say to the daughter of Zion, 'Behold your

King is coming to you, gentle, and mounted on a
donkey, even on a colt, the foal of a beast of burden.'"

The disciples went and did just as Jesus had
instructed them, and brought the donkey and the
colt, and laid their coats on them; and He sat on
the coats. Most of the crowd spread their coats in
the road, and others were cutting branches from
the trees and spreading them in the road. The
crowds going ahead of Him, and those who followed, were shouting, "Hosanna to the Son of
David; blessed is He who comes in the name of
the Lord; hosanna in the highest!"

In fulfillment of Zechariah 9:9, Yeshua's entry into
Jerusalem on a lowly donkey reveals His unconditional
love for us. He rode in, knowing that days later the
shouts of "Hosanna!" would turn into "Crucify Him!"

## 16. MESSIAH WILL INITIALLY BE REJECTED BY THE PEOPLE OF ISRAEL

The rejection of Messiah by His own people would not
invalidate Him; rather, it would serve to verify that He
is indeed the Messiah, the rejected One of whom the
prophet Isaiah foretold. Isaiah 53 graphically spells out
the rejection Messiah would bear:

Who has believed our message? And to whom has
the arm of the LORD been revealed? For He grew
up before Him like a tender shoot, and like a root
out of parched ground; He has no stately form
or majesty that we should look upon Him, nor

appearance that we should be attracted to Him. *He was despised and forsaken of men, a man of sorrows and acquainted with grief; and like one from whom men hide their face He was despised, and we did not esteem Him.*

Surely our griefs He Himself bore, and our sorrows He carried; yet we ourselves esteemed Him stricken, smitten of God, and afflicted. But He was pierced through for our transgressions, He was crushed for our iniquities; the chastening for our well-being fell upon Him, and by His scourging we are healed. All of us like sheep have gone astray, each of us has turned to his own way; but the LORD has caused the iniquity of us all to fall on Him.

He was oppressed and He was afflicted, yet He did not open His mouth; like a lamb that is led to slaughter, and like a sheep that is silent before its shearers, so He did not open His mouth. By oppression and judgment He was taken away; and as for His generation, who considered that He was cut off out of the land of the living for the transgression of my people, to whom the stroke was due? His grave was assigned with wicked men, yet He was with a rich man in His death, because He had done no violence, nor was there any deceit in His mouth.

But the LORD was pleased to crush Him, putting Him to grief; if He would render Himself as a guilt offering, He will see His offspring, He will prolong His days, and the good pleasure of the LORD will prosper in His hand. As a result of the anguish of His soul, He will see it and be satisfied;

by His knowledge the Righteous One, My Servant, will justify the many, as He will bear their iniquities. Therefore, I will allot Him a portion with the great, and He will divide the booty with the strong; because He poured out Himself to death, and was numbered with the transgressors; yet He Himself bore the sin of many, and interceded for the transgressors.

—ISAIAH 53:1–12, EMPHASIS ADDED

The tragedy and horror of Messiah's experience of being despised and rejected by His people is captured in John 1:11, *"He came to His own, and those who were His own did not receive Him"* (emphasis added). It is even more graphically presented in Matthew 27, when Pilate sought to save Jesus but the Jewish crowd cried out in unison, "Crucify Him!"

While he was sitting on the judgment seat, his wife sent him a message, saying, "Have nothing to do with that righteous Man; for last night I suffered greatly in a dream because of Him." But the chief priests and the elders persuaded the crowds to ask for Barabbas and to put Jesus to death. But the governor said to them, "Which of the two do you want me to release for you?" And they said, "Barabbas." Pilate said to them, "Then what shall I do with Jesus who is called Christ?" They all said, "Crucify Him!" And he said, "Why, what evil has He done?" But they kept shouting all the more, saying, "Crucify Him!"

When Pilate saw that he was accomplishing

nothing, but rather that a riot was starting, he took water and washed his hands in front of the crowd, saying, "I am innocent of this Man's blood; see to that yourselves."

—MATTHEW 27:19–24

## 17. MESSIAH WILL BE CRUCIFIED

Yeshua's rejection culminated in His crucifixion, which was prophesied in Psalm 22.

I am poured out like water, and all my bones are out of joint; my heart is like wax; it is melted within me. My strength is dried up like a potsherd, and my tongue cleaves to my jaws; and You lay me in the dust of death. For dogs have surrounded me; a band of evildoers has encompassed me; *they pierced my hands and my feet.*

—PSALM 22:14–16, EMPHASIS ADDED

We see the fulfillment highlighted in John 20 when Jesus appeared to His disciples after His resurrection. The nail prints in Yeshua's hands were the proof the disciples needed to believe He was truly the Messiah whose crucifixion they had witnessed just days before.

And when He had said this, He showed them both His hands and His side. The disciples then rejoiced when they saw the Lord....But Thomas, one of the twelve, called Didymus, was not with them when Jesus came. So the other disciples were saying to him, "We have seen the Lord!" But he said to them, *"Unless I see in His hands the*

> *imprint of the nails, and put my finger into the*
> *place of the nails,* and put my hand into His side,
> I will not believe."
> —JOHN 20:20, 24–25, EMPHASIS ADDED

After Yeshua's death by crucifixion, the soldiers divided up His garments, which was also prophesied in Psalm 22: "They *divide my garments* among them, and for my clothing they cast lots" (v. 18, emphasis added). We see this come to pass in Matthew 27:35 exactly as Psalm 22 described: "And when they had crucified Him, *they divided up His garments* among themselves by casting lots" (emphasis added).

Amazingly, Messianic prophecy also anticipated the circumstances surrounding Jesus' burial. Isaiah prophesied that Yeshua would be buried with a rich man: "His grave was assigned with wicked men, yet *He was with a rich man in His death*, because He had done no violence, nor was there any deceit in His mouth" (Isa. 53:9, emphasis added). This was fulfilled when a rich man named Joseph of Arimathea buried Yeshua's body in a tomb he had made for himself.

> When it was evening, there came a rich man from Arimathea, named Joseph, who himself had also become a disciple of Jesus. This man went to Pilate and asked for the body of Jesus. Then Pilate ordered it to be given to him. *And Joseph took the body and wrapped it in a clean linen cloth, and laid it in his own new tomb,* which he had hewn

out in the rock; and he rolled a large stone against
the entrance of the tomb and went away.
—MATTHEW 27:57–60, EMPHASIS ADDED

The circumstances surrounding Yeshua's death—that
He would be crucified, His clothes would be divided up,
and He would be buried in a rich man's tomb—were all
foreseen deep within the pages of the Old Testament.

## 18. MESSIAH WILL RISE FROM THE DEAD

Wondrously, even the resurrection of Messiah Yeshua is
etched deep within the pages of the Hebrew Scriptures.
We see it glimpsed in Psalm 16:9–11: "Therefore my heart
is glad and my glory rejoices; my flesh also will dwell
securely. *For You will not abandon my soul to Sheol; nor
will You allow Your Holy One to undergo decay.* You will
make known to me the path of life; in Your presence is
fullness of joy; in Your right hand there are pleasures
forever" (emphasis added).

On the day of Pentecost, while proclaiming to the
Jewish people that Yeshua was the Messiah of Israel, Peter
quoted directly from Psalm 16:9–11, claiming Yeshua
fulfilled it. Here is Peter's sermon as recorded in Acts
2:22–32 (emphasis added):

> Men of Israel, listen to these words: Jesus the
> Nazarene, a man attested to you by God with
> miracles and wonders and signs which God per-
> formed through Him in your midst, just as you
> yourselves know—this Man, delivered over by the
> predetermined plan and foreknowledge of God,

you nailed to a cross by the hands of godless men and put Him to death. But God raised Him up again, putting an end to the agony of death, since it was impossible for Him to be held in its power.

For David says of Him, "I saw the Lord always in my presence; for He is at my right hand, so that I will not be shaken. Therefore my heart was glad and my tongue exulted; moreover my flesh also will live in hope; because *You will not abandon my soul to Hades, nor allow Your Holy One to undergo decay.* You have made known to me the ways of life; You will make me full of gladness with Your presence."

Brethren, I may confidently say to you regarding the patriarch David that he both died and was buried, and his tomb is with us to this day. And so, because he was a prophet and knew that God had sworn to him with an oath to seat one of his descendants on his throne, he looked ahead and spoke of the resurrection of the Christ, that He was neither abandoned to Hades, nor did His flesh suffer decay. This Jesus God raised up again, to which we are all witnesses.

## 19. Messiah Will Bring Israel to Salvation

Hebrew prophecy anticipates and records both the initial resistance of the Jewish people to the Messiah as well as their subsequent remorse and repentance, resulting in their salvation. Zechariah 12:10 says, "I will pour out on the house of David and on the inhabitants of Jerusalem, the Spirit of grace and of supplication, so that they will look on Me whom they have pierced; and they will mourn for Him, as one mourns for an only son, and they will weep bitterly over Him like the bitter weeping over a first-born." They will weep precisely because they will finally see Yeshua for who He truly is. Zechariah 13:1 describes this glorious day and tells us, "*In that day a fountain will be opened for the house of David and for the inhabitants of Jerusalem, for sin and for impurity*" (emphasis added).

Paul picks this theme up in Romans 11:25–27: "For I do not want you, brethren, to be uninformed of this mystery—so that you will not be wise in your own estimation—that a partial hardening has happened to Israel until the fullness of the Gentiles has come in; and so all Israel will be saved; just as it is written, '*The Deliverer will come from Zion, He will remove ungodliness from Jacob. This is My covenant with them, when I take away their sins*'" (emphasis added).

## 20. MESSIAH WILL COME AGAIN

In the same way the Hebrew Bible anticipated the first coming of Yeshua, it also anticipated His second coming.

Daniel had an incredible and mysterious vision foreshadowing the glorification of the Messiah, who is the Son of Man: "I kept looking in the night visions, and behold, with the clouds of heaven one like a Son of Man was coming, and He came up to the Ancient of Days and was presented before Him. And to Him was given dominion, glory and a kingdom, that all the peoples, nations and men of every language might serve Him. His dominion is an everlasting dominion which will not pass away; and His kingdom is one which will not be destroyed" (Dan. 7:13–14).

The glorious fulfillment of Daniel's prophecy will be wholly and irreversibly realized at Yeshua's return. Hear the words of Jesus Himself:

> But in those days, after that tribulation, the sun will be darkened and the moon will not give its light, and the stars will be falling from heaven, and the powers that are in the heavens will be shaken. Then they will see the Son of Man coming in clouds with great power and glory.
>
> —MARK 13:24–26

> For the Son of Man is going to come in the glory of His Father with His angels, and will then repay every man according to his deeds.
>
> —MATTHEW 16:27

## 21. MESSIAH WILL BRING US INTO UNION WITH GOD

At the end of the day, the examination of fulfilled Messianic prophecies alone is not enough to bring salvation. Living faith is the gift of God and is produced by God's Spirit supernaturally. (See Ephesians 2:8.)

There will always be parts of the Bible and things in life that we do not understand. Faith gives us the wings to rise above what we do not understand to trust in a God whose ways are above our ways and whose thoughts are above our thoughts (Isa. 55:9). Seeing Messianic prophecy fulfilled absolutely strengthens our faith, but at the end of the day, we have to come to a place on the inside that through our own personal experience we have found that God is real, He loves us, and we can trust Him.

The Lord said through the prophet Jeremiah, "You will seek Me and find Me when you search for Me with all your heart" (Jer. 29:13), and through the prophet Ezekiel, "I will put My Spirit within you and cause you to walk in My statutes, and you will be careful to observe My ordinances" (Ezek. 36:27). After walking with Messiah Jesus for over forty years, I can tell you that He has made Himself real to me over and over and over and over again. The ancient prophecies of the Messiah have been fulfilled in my own heart.

As I close, I want to leave you with this challenge. If you're not fully convinced Jesus is the Messiah, put His words in John 7:17 to the test: "If anyone is willing to do His will, he will know of the teaching, whether it is of God or whether I speak from Myself." In other words, Jesus is saying, "If you will open your heart to Me and obey Me, you will experience My reality and know that I am the Messiah."

# Notes

### CHAPTER 4

1. *Encyclopaedia Britannica*, s.v. "Antiochus IV Epiphanes," accessed July 15, 2022, https://www.britannica.com/biography/Antiochus-IV-Epiphanes.

### CHAPTER 9

1. Blue Letter Bible, s.v. "Why Is the Bible Divided Into Chapters and Verses?," accessed July 13, 2022, https://www.blueletterbible.org/Comm/stewart_don/faq/bible-special/question8-why-is-the-bible-divided-into-chapters-and-verses.cfm.
2. Bible Hub, s.v. *"choli,"* accessed July 13, 2022, https://biblehub.com/hebrew/2483.htm.
3. Bible Hub, s.v. *"makob,"* accessed July 13, 2022, https://biblehub.com/hebrew/4341.htm.
4. Leanna Cinquanta, *Treasures in Dark Places* (Bloomington, MN: Chosen Books, 2017), 93–95.

### CHAPTER 11

1. David B. Green, "This Day in Jewish History—3761 BCE: The World Is Created, According to the Hebrew Calendar and an Obscure Sage," *Haaretz*, October 7, 2015, https://www.haaretz.com/jewish/2015-10-07/ty-article/3761-bce-the-world-is-created/0000017f-e4be-d7b2-a77f-e7bf482b0000.

# DISCOVERING THE JEWISH JESUS

## CONNECT WITH RABBI SCHNEIDER

www.DiscoveringTheJewishJesus.com

 /Discovering the Jewish Jesus with Rabbi Schneider

 facebook.com/rabbischneider

 @RabbiSchneider

Roku—Discovering the Jewish Jesus

Apple TV—Discovering the Jewish Jesus

 Amazon App—Discovering the Jewish Jesus

 Podcast—Discovering the Jewish Jesus

Search for Rabbi Schneider and Discovering the Jewish Jesus on your favorite platform.

For a complete list of Rabbi Schneider's television and radio broadcasts, visit www.DiscoveringTheJewishJesus.com.